CONTENTS

6   CHAPTER 1
Growing Up Kennedy

38   CHAPTER 2
From the South Pacific to the Senate

74   CHAPTER 3
Family Man and Modern Campaigner

110   CHAPTER 4
"Let the Word Go Forth . . . "

134   CHAPTER 5
Leader of the Free World

156   CHAPTER 6
The Legacy

173   Credits

174   Bibliography

176   About the Author and Acknowledgments

GROWING UP KENNEDY

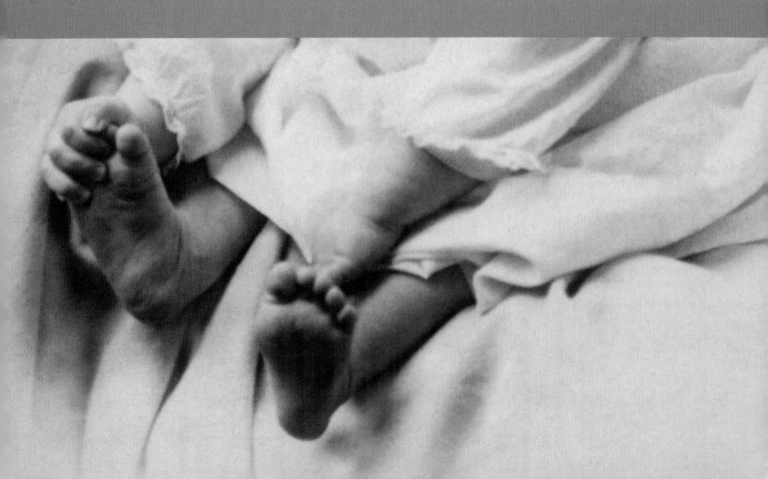

1.

WANTED—A good, reliable woman to take the care of a boy two years old, in a small family in Brookline. Good wages and a permanent situation given. No washing or ironing will be required, but good recommendations as to character and capacity demanded. Postively no Irish need apply. Call at 224 Washington street, corner of Summer street.
6t   jy 28

SHORTLY AFTER 3:00 P.M. on May 29, 1917, John Fitzgerald Kennedy entered the world in a modest wood-frame home at 83 Beals Street in the Boston suburb of Brookline, Massachusetts.

Both of his parents, Joseph Kennedy and Rose Fitzgerald Kennedy, descended from the wave of Irish immigrants who poured into Boston in the mid-19th century aboard miserably disease-ridden boats called "coffin ships," fleeing a potato famine that claimed one million Irish lives. As the first big wave of immigrants to America's shores, the Irish faced intense discrimination from the native-born Protestants of Anglo-Saxon stock. The Irish were Roman Catholics—"Papists" in the parlance of the day—in an overwhelmingly Protestant land. They were regarded as prone to drunkenness, brawling, and thieving.

"Help wanted" ads in newspapers often ended with "no Irish need apply." America was a young country in need of labor, however. The Irish dug a foothold for themselves through sheer hard work, and they advanced using their flair for politics. In the teeth of prejudice, both the Kennedys and the Fitzgeralds managed to prosper in business and political arenas.

Joseph Kennedy's grandparents had arrived in America with nothing but the clothes on their backs. Their son, Patrick (Joe's father), scrimped and saved to buy a saloon and eventually became a state assemblyman. By the time Joe was born in 1888, Patrick owned a bank. Young Joe attended Boston Latin School and Harvard along with the city's Protestant elite, but despite his comfortable upbringing and first-class education, he would nurse resentment against the established order. He lived his life determined to prove that he—and later his children—were not only as good as anyone

LEFT A six-month-old Jack beams at the camera in this photo taken at the family's home in Brookline, 1917.

ABOVE A newspaper job listing showing the explicit prejudice Irish immigrants faced in their adopted homeland.

else, but *better*. "Always come first. Second place is failure," he liked to say—a phrase that succinctly sums up Joe's intensely competitive, contentious personality.

As a boy and young man, Joe had two great loves—playing sports and making money. At Harvard, he was an indifferent student. Rather than focusing on his studies, Joe, along with a friend, ran a horse-drawn tour bus service that pulled in about $5,000 a year. After graduation, he became a bank examiner, and by 1913, at age twenty-five, he managed with some help from family money to gain control of the Columbia Trust Bank. This accomplishment gave him the opportunity to boast to anyone in earshot that he was "the youngest bank president in the country."

LEFT Joe Sr. spent most of his baseball career at Harvard on the bench, but still managed to earn a letter in the sport.
ABOVE Joe, self-proclaimed "America's youngest bank president," poses at his desk at the Columbia Trust Bank.

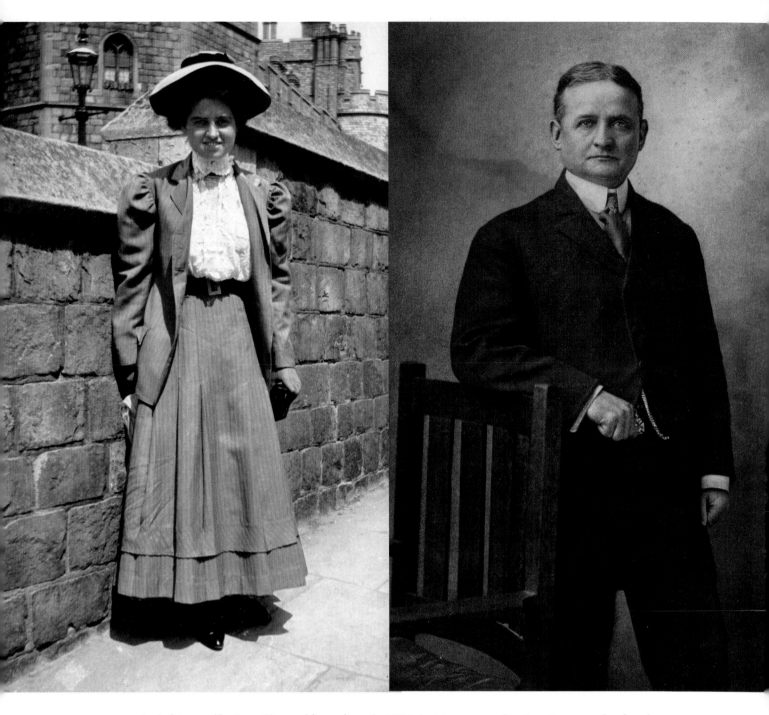

Joe's future wife, Rose Fitzgerald, was born in 1890, just two years after Joe. Rose was the daughter of John F. "Honey Fitz" Fitzgerald—so nicknamed for his charm as well as his habit of bursting into song at the slightest provocation ("Sweet Adeline" was his signature tune). In a long and sometimes scandal-plagued political career, "Honey Fitz" served twice as Boston's mayor, plus stints as a representative in Massachusetts's state house and in Congress.

Like Joe Kennedy, Rose led a privileged childhood, including time at a private school in Europe. She wanted to attend Wellesley College and become a schoolteacher, but Honey Fitz decided that it wouldn't sit well with his Irish and Italian constituents in Boston's North End if his daughter attended a Protestant college. So instead, she went to the College of the Sacred Heart in Manhattanville, New York.

Joe and Rose met as children at Old Orchard Beach, Maine—a favorite resort of Boston's affluent "lace-curtain Irish" families—and after a long courtship, he proposed to her in 1914. At first, Honey Fitz was opposed to the match: He had his eye on another young man as a more "suitable" husband for

Rose. But Joe's growing success as a banker finally convinced him, and he relented. The couple married on October 7, 1914. Their first child, Joseph Kennedy Jr., arrived on July 28, 1915. He was the first of nine children that Joe Sr. and Rose would produce.

By the time Jack was born, the United States had entered World War I. Joe Sr. didn't serve in the military. Instead, he worked as the manager of a shipyard in Quincy, Massachusetts. In later years, some of Joe Sr.'s political enemies accused him of "dodging the draft," but his job was important to the war effort. True to form, though, he made money on the side by selling coffee and sandwiches to his own workers. After the war ended, he became a stockbroker.

FAR LEFT Rose in Ireland during a year studying abroad, 1908. CENTER John Francis "Honey Fitz" Fitzgerald, captured in a rare solemn moment. ABOVE Members of the Fitzgerald and Kennedy clans at Old Orchard Beach, Maine, where Boston's wealthy and powerful Irish-American families retreated on vacation.

JACK'S GENERATION

Joe Sr. spent the 1920s turning his already considerable fortune into an immense one. By 1925, he'd achieved his goal of becoming a millionaire. He made his money by exploiting three things that obsessed Americans in the 1920s: booze, movies, and the stock market.

Prohibition was the law of the land from 1920–1933, but millions of Americans were still thirsty. Joe Sr. recognized this, and he found a legal means of providing alcohol to people. Rather than take the route of a traditional bootlegger, who smuggled liquor into the country or produced it at illegal stills, he purchased interests in companies that produced alcoholic beverages for "medicinal and religious" purposes. Of course, a lot of this alcohol found its way into hands that didn't belong to physicians or clergy. He also warehoused huge stocks of liquor and negotiated importation contracts in anticipation of the day Prohibition would be repealed, and he made a killing when that day came in 1933.

Joe Sr. was also quick to see Hollywood's profit potential. Starting with the purchase of a movie-distributing agency in 1926, Joe Sr. became a prime mover in the creation of RKO, a major movie studio and movie-theater chain. This involvement in the film industry would be an important entrée for Jack to the social world of Hollywood in the 1940s.

LEFT Rose in her white satin wedding gown, 1914. Befitting the couple's social position, the ceremony was held in the cardinal of the Archdiocese of Boston's private residence. ABOVE From financier and industrialist to movie mogul: Joe Sr. with cowboy star Tom Mix at the start of a publicity tour, circa 1926.

All the while, Joe Sr. speculated heavily and successfully in the ever-rising stock market of the late 1920s. The financial markets were poorly regulated in those days, so it was hard to identify any dealings as "insider trading." With suspiciously perfect timing, Joe Sr. pulled his money out of stocks just before the New York Stock Exchange crashed in 1929. He claimed a Wall Street shoeshine boy had told him that the bubble was about to burst. The crisis that sparked the Great Depression and wiped out the savings of millions of Americans left Joe Sr. richer than before.

For Joe Sr., making money wasn't just a measure of success; it was a means to an end—the advancement of the Kennedys up the political and social ladder. Joe Sr. reportedly told friends he wanted to give each of his nine children one million dollars so that none of them would have to work. Freed from the need to make money, the younger generation would be expected to spend their time achieving great things.

Joe Sr.'s wide-ranging interests meant frequent absences from home—and many infidelities. In addition to dalliances with showgirls and secretaries, he had a long affair with actress Gloria Swanson and may have even briefly considered leaving Rose for her. Rose took the Church's command that sex was only for procreation quite literally, and after the birth of Teddy in 1932, she shut her bedroom door. Joe Sr. used Rose's strict adherence to Catholic doctrine to rationalize his philandering.

Rose was a dutiful parent, toting a card file listing the children's medical histories, lining them up for regular doses of cod-liver oil, and posting a schedule of the next day's activities each night. But she hardly exuded maternal warmth. A grown-up Jack would remark to a friend, "My mother never hugged me . . . never!" However, Rose's coldness may not have been entirely a product of her personality. Several biographers have noted that Dr. L. Emmett Holt's popular book, *The Care and Feeding of Children*, instructed parents in the 1910s and 1920s to minimize physical contact with their offspring so as not to spread disease.

While she was a very involved mother, Rose did spend a considerable amount of time away from home, leaving the children in the care of servants. Sometimes her destination was Paris, where she pursued her other great solace—*haute couture*. Once, when six-year-old Jack learned that Rose was packing for another trip, he confronted her: "Gee, you're a great mother to go away and leave your children all alone!" Rose brushed him off, thinking Jack was just being "cute."

Rose may have been "the glue that held our family together," as Jack later said, but Joe Sr. was its emotional heart. Rose made sure the kids took their medicine, but Joe Sr. challenged them. Around the dinner table, for example, Joe Sr. quizzed the children about current events. They were expected to know what was going on in the world and to comment intelligently.

Soon it became apparent that one Kennedy sibling couldn't keep up: Rosemary. It was clear not long after her birth that she was lagging behind in mental development. She learned to read and write, but only with great difficulty. She probably suffered from severe dyslexia, a condition little understood at the time. When she was young, her sweet nature endeared her to everyone. However, in her early

RIGHT The next generation in his arms, Joe Sr. poses with Joe Jr. (left) and Jack.

twenties, her personality underwent alarming changes. She began to suffer from mood swings and erratic behavior, sometimes storming out of the house.

Joe Sr. hoped that a newly developed medical procedure—the lobotomy—would stabilize Rosemary. The operation involved inserting a sharp instrument into the frontal lobe of the brain. Frontal lobotomies were delicate and often hazardous operations that could result in severe mental disabilities. The procedure reduced Rosemary, in biographer Geoffrey Perret's words, "to the mentality of a four-year-old." She was packed off to a Catholic-run home for the disabled in Wisconsin. Rosemary was a family secret for years, and it wasn't until Jack ran for president in 1960 that the family finally acknowledged her condition. Rosemary would die in the home in Wisconsin in 2005. Her condition led the Kennedys to contribute generously to charities for the mentally disabled.

ABOVE Joe Jr. (second from right), Jack (second from left), and friends in the water off the family "compound" in Hyannis Port, Massachusetts, circa 1925. RIGHT The expressions on the faces of Joe Jr. (left) and Jack capture both their closeness and their competiveness as brothers and rivals.

After Joe Jr., Jack, and Rosemary, the Kennedy brood eventually grew to nine, with Kathleen (b. 1920), Eunice (b. 1921), Patricia (b. 1924), Robert (b. 1925), Jean (b. 1928), and finally Edward (b. 1932).

Jack had an especially close relationship with the equally high-spirited Kathleen—nicknamed "Kick"—but the sibling dynamic that dominated his boyhood and early manhood was his rivalry with Joe Jr., who never let Jack forget that *he* was the first-born. The obvious apple of both their parents' eyes, and the one marked out to lead, he liked to remind his siblings, "When Dad's not home, I'm the boss!" The two eldest boys were intensely competitive. On one occasion, Joe Sr. suggested his sons have a bike race, and they wound up deliberately ramming each other, leading to stitches.

While his competitiveness never ceased, Jack likely grasped at an early age that he was forever at a disadvantage. His older brother was bigger, better looking, and a better athlete. Joe Jr. was also a go-along-to-get-along kind of guy who had a knack for living up to everyone's expectations, seemingly effortlessly. Perhaps in response to this, Jack was a bit of a rebel and a wise guy from an early age. Young Jack was ostentatiously sloppy in his dress and appearance. Photos from his school days often show him with a shirttail out or an oddly knotted tie, his hair—which turned from red to brown as he grew up—in an unruly tangle. It was as if Jack was already asserting himself as an individual—not to be seen as simply Joe Jr.'s little brother or, for that matter, the son of Joe Sr.

Jack's devil-may-care attitude toward social conventions didn't end with childhood. When he came home from World War II a hero, an exasperated Rose wrote in a family letter, "He is just the same. He wears his oldest clothes, still late for meals, still [carries] no money. He has even overflowed the bathtub."

For all their rivalry, there was a close bond between Jack and Joe Jr. When they worked together—such as in sailing regattas, a passion for both boys—they were formidable. Doris Kearns Goodwin observed that Joe Jr. was a kind of "protective shield" for Jack, because "everything was expected of the older brother . . ." The knowledge that all eyes were focused on Joe Jr. gave Jack some breathing room.

EDUCATING JACK

Jack attended private schools in Boston until 1927, when Joe Sr., feeling that he'd gone as far as he could in Boston, moved the family to New York. They first lived on the Hudson River–side enclave of Riverdale in the Bronx, then moved to Bronxville, an affluent Westchester County suburb. He would later acquire vacation homes for the family in Palm Beach, Florida, and Hyannis Port, Massachusetts.

In 1930, Jack was sent to Canterbury, a Catholic prep school in Connecticut, to ready him for the elite Choate School, where Joe Jr. was in attendance. In May 1931, at the end of his second year at Canterbury, Jack came down with appendicitis and had to undergo an emergency operation. In fact, Jack's health problems were chronic, to put it mildly. He suffered from a number of congenital ailments: hives, blurred vision, constant colds and fevers, and an inability to put on weight. While he recovered well from his appendectomy, Jack's academic and professional life would come to be dominated by health concerns, many of which were disclosed only to those closest to him.

It took Jack a couple of tries to pass Choate's entrance exams, but he was eventually admitted, and he began school in October 1931. Jack was a middling student, excelling in subjects he enjoyed, like English, and scraping by in the rest, like foreign languages. By now, he'd become an avid reader, although most of the books he read didn't appear in Choate's curriculum. One day, he amazed a friend by correctly answering most of the questions on a radio quiz show. "I guess I read a lot," he said.

Jack was also an irrepressible joker and prankster, and he collected a circle of friends with the same priorities, including LeMoyne Billings. "Lem" practically worshiped Jack, and he became a kind of Sancho Panza to Jack's Don Quixote. Lem remained a close friend, confidant, and unofficial adviser for the rest of Jack's life.

Jack's irreverence ultimately led Choate's headmaster to call a school-wide meeting in which he struck out at Jack, Lem, and their cronies. He called them "muckers," a reference to people who sweep

LEFT The Kennedy clan at its full, final complement, photographed in Bronxville, 1937. ABOVE On their way to adulthood in long pants and ties, Joe Jr. (left) and Jack with their father at the Kennedy's winter headquarters at Palm Beach, 1931.

the dung out of stables. Jack was delighted rather than chastened, and he ordered up rings engraved with the initials CMC—for "Choate Muckers Club"—to give to his crew. When the headmaster got word of the rings, he told the group of boys that they were all expelled. It turned out to be a bluff, but Joe Sr. had to come up from New York to talk some sense into his second son.

ABOVE Jack (far right) and fellow members of the Choate "Muckers Club." Lem Billings, Jack's lifelong friend and confidant, is second from left between Ralph Horton and Butch Shriber. RIGHT Choate's Christmas cut-ups: Ralph, Lem, and Jack (left to right) sent out this Christmas card under the nicknames "Rip," "Leem," and "Ken."

We're puttin' on our top hat,
   Tyin' up our white tie,
         Brushin' off our tails,

In order to
   Wish you

A Merry Christmas

Rip,   Leem,   Ken.

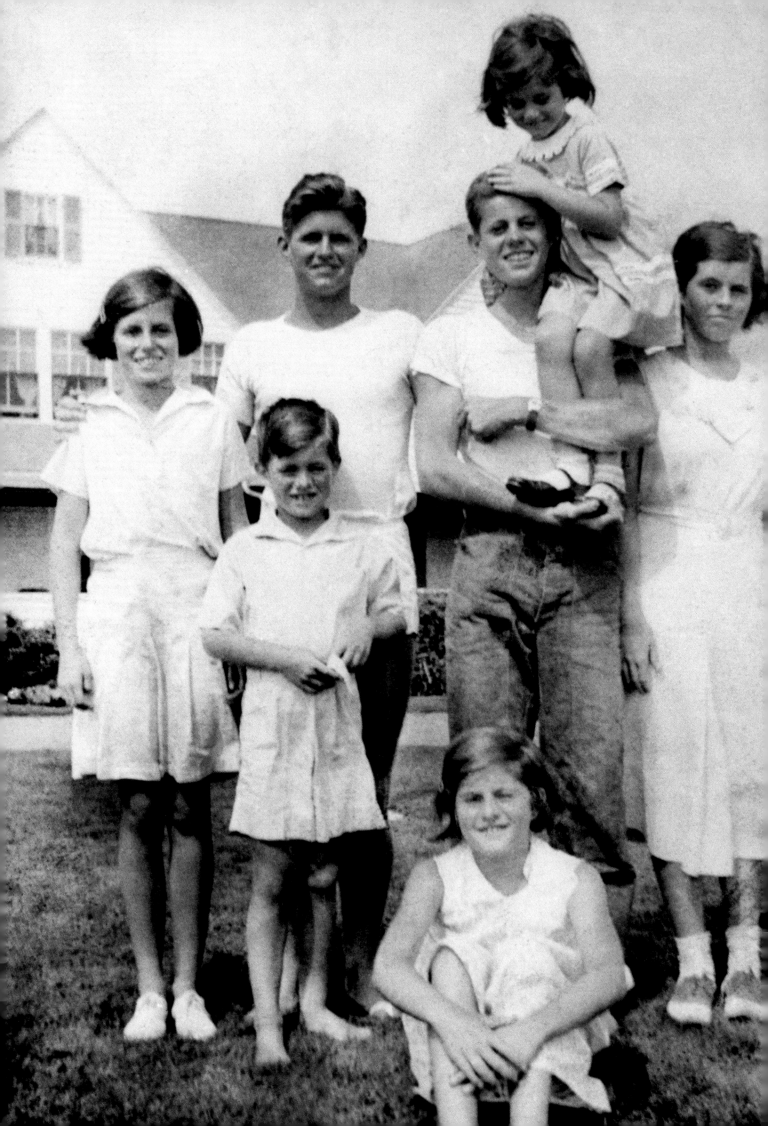

HARVARD AND THE COURT OF ST. JAMES

Having spent much of his time at Choate in Joe Jr.'s shadow, Jack had no desire to repeat the process

at Harvard after he graduated from Choate in 1935. He opted instead to follow Lem Billings to

Princeton. Joe Sr., however, insisted that Jack first spend a year of study with the celebrated British

academic Sir Harold Laski at the London School of Economics. Joe Jr. had spent his pre-Harvard

LEFT Seven of the nine Kennedy kids, circa mid-1930s. ABOVE Jack with a football at the Bronxville property,
1936. Some guests dreaded being dragged into the Kennedy men's notoriously rough touch-football games.

I solemnly swear that the statements made on both sides of this application are true and that the photograph attached hereto is a likeness of me.

OATH OF ALLEGIANCE

Further, I do solemnly swear that I will support and defend the Constitution of the United States against all enemies, foreign and domestic; that I will bear true faith and allegiance to the same; and that I take this obligation freely, without any mental reservation or purpose of evasion: So help me God.

John F. Kennedy
(Signature of applicant)

SEP 17 1935

Subscribed and sworn to before me this _____ day of _____, 193____

_____
Clerk of the _____ Court at ____ N. Y. City
Agent, Department of State

DESCRIPTION OF APPLICANT

Height: **5** feet, **11** inches. Age: **18** years.

Hair: **Brown**

Eyes: **Green**

Distinguishing marks or features: _____
(Note any facial marks or scars by which applicant may be identified)

Place of birth: **BROOKLINE, MASS**
(City and State)

Date of birth: **MAY 29 1917**
(Month, day, and year)

Occupation: **STUDENT**

I intend to leave the United States from the port of **NEW YORK CITY**
(Port of departure)

sailing on board the **NORMANDIE** on **SEPTEMBER 25**, 193**5**
(Name of ship)   (Date of departure)

ADDRESS

I request that my passport be mailed to the following address:

Name: **JOHN F. KENNEDY**

No. and Street: **ROOM 4437 - 30 ROCKEFELLER PLAZA**

City and State: **NEW YORK, N. Y.**

[NOTE.—A passport will not be mailed to an hotel address unless the hotel is the applicant's place of permanent residence.]

AFFIDAVIT OF IDENTIFYING WITNESS

I, the undersigned, solemnly swear that I am a citizen of the United States; that I reside at the address written below my signature hereto affixed; that I know the applicant who executed the affidavit hereinbefore set forth to be a citizen of the United States; that the statements made herein by the applicant are true to the best of my knowledge and belief; further, I solemnly swear that I have known the applicant personally for **Five** years.

If witness has been issued a passport, give number and date of issue or approximate date of issue.

P J Murphy
(Signature of witness)

2800 Bailey Ave NYC
(Residence address of witness)

No. ____ Date of issue ____

No lawyer or other person will be accepted as witness to a passport application if he has received or expects to receive a fee for his services in connection with the execution of the application or obtaining the passport.

SEP 17 1935

Subscribed and sworn to before me this ____ day of _____, 193____

_____
Agent, Department of State, N. Y. City
Clerk of the _____ Court

at _____

[SEAL OR COURT]

Two photographs (duplicates) are required; one to be affixed to the application in the space designated above, and the other bearing the signature of the applicant, to accompany the application unattached. A group photograph should be used if more than one person is to be included in the passport. Photographs must be on thin paper, should have a light background, and be not over 3 by 3 inches nor less than 2½ by 2½ inches in size.

A person born in the United States should submit a birth or baptismal certificate with his application, or if a birth or baptismal certificate is not obtainable, affidavits from the attending physician, parents, or other persons having sufficient knowledge to be able to testify as to the date and place of the applicant's birth should be submitted. The same kind of evidence should be submitted if American-born wife is included in the application and the marriage occurred on or after September 22, 1922. If he acquired American citizenship through naturalization on or after date just mentioned, evidence of her citizenship of the nature set forth in the PASSPORT REGULATIONS should be submitted.

U.S. GOVERNMENT PRINTING OFFICE: 1934   1—1149

year at LSE. Jack sailed for Europe in the summer of 1945 on his first overseas trip. He lasted a week at the LSE before contracting jaundice and being sent back to the States. He entered Princeton in November—only to wind up in the hospital again. The doctors still couldn't determine just what was wrong with him, but when his white blood cell count shot up, they suspected a truly serious and deadly disease: leukemia. "They were mentally measuring me for a coffin," Jack told his pal Billings.

In the winter of 1935, Jack was packed off to a ranch in Benson, Arizona, where he worked as a "hired hand" for $1.00 a day—the first money he'd ever earned by his own labor. The sun, the hard work, and the clear air seemed to improve his health; he appeared fitter and stronger.

Jack elected to enter Harvard in the fall of 1936 rather than return to Princeton. He focused more on athletics than academics in his freshman and sophomore years. As at Choate, his grades were unexceptional and his attitude toward studying remained casual: "Exam today, so have to open my book and see . . . what the course is about," he wrote to Billings during semester finals. He made the freshman football team, where his coach would recall, "he played for keeps." But carrying 150 pounds on a six-foot frame, he was simply too light to have much traction on the gridiron. At some point during this time, he may have suffered a football injury that led to the back problems that would plague him for the rest of his life. He did better on the swim team, where backstroke was his specialty.

At the end of the academic year, Joe Sr., who like many knowledgeable Americans and Europeans was convinced that another war in Europe loomed, told Jack he should see the continent "before the

LEFT Jack's passport application, filed prior to his trip to Europe in 1935. The bow tie he wears in the photo was a rare feature in his laid-back attire. ABOVE Joe Sr. and Joe Jr. are absent from this Kennedy family photo, with Joe Sr. likely in England and Joe Jr. at Harvard when it was taken.

shooting starts." So in June 1937, Jack sailed for Europe on the ocean liner *George Washington,* bringing along Lem Billings and a Ford convertible.

The two piloted the Ford through France, Italy, Germany, and the Netherlands. They made the usual rounds of cathedrals, castles, ruins, and museums, and had the kind of adventures and misadventures a couple of high-spirited young men were bound to have on a road trip through Europe. Everywhere they went, Jack made a point of meeting with local people and questioning them closely, including refugees from the Spanish Civil War in southern France and pro- and anti-Nazi hitchhikers in Germany.

This trip, too, was plagued by Jack's health problems. Toward the end of the trip, his back pain reached the point that he had to relinquish the wheel to Billings full-time. And when they reached London, he was hospitalized for several days, possibly due to an allergic reaction to a dachshund puppy they'd bought along the way.

ABOVE Jack feeds the famous pigeons in Venice's St. Mark's Square, summer 1937. RIGHT Jack and Lem in Europe with the dachshund puppy they named Dunker. Jack proclaimed the pup a dog of "great beauty."

Jack returned to Harvard as a junior in 1937, at a time when the great countries he'd just toured were on the brink of war. Joe Sr. recognized this, and he lobbied hard for a diplomatic posting that would place him in an influential position at the center of the action. At the end of that year, President Franklin Roosevelt appointed Joe Sr. as the United States ambassador to the Court of St. James (Britain). The position was America's most prestigious diplomatic posting. Joe saw that, having achieved fantastic wealth and significant political influence, this was the best next step in advancing his family's social stature. Joe Sr., Rose, and the younger children arrived in London in March 1938.

Enclosure

Jack kept a meticulous diary of his 1937 trip to Europe, filling pages with thoughtful analyses of the continent's social, political, and economic problems. He estimated that ninety-five percent of Americans had no real idea of what was going on in Europe.

ABOVE Joe Sr. (left) shakes hands with President Roosevelt after his swearing-in as ambassador to the Court of St. James, 1938. U.S. Supreme Court Justice Stanley F. Reed looks on. RIGHT Jack tries his hand at juggling in Nuremberg, Germany, the city that hosted the Nazi party's immense rallies. Jack was impressed and appalled by the Nazis' brilliant use of spectacle and propaganda.

The Kennedy clan was a big hit with the British press and public. The papers nicknamed the new ambassador "Jolly Joe," noted with approval that Joe Sr. and Rose got on well with King George VI and Queen Mary, and printed glowing articles about the handsome, vigorous family.

But the honeymoon didn't last long. Throwing diplomatic discretion to the wind, Joe Sr. soon made it clear he sided with the mostly right-wing, upper-class Britons who favored a policy of appeasement, making deals with Nazi Germany rather than standing up to it. To Joe Sr., it was simple: War with Germany was coming. Britain, France, and the few remaining European democracies couldn't hope to defeat Germany in a war, and he didn't want the United States to get dragged into what he thought would be a hopeless conflict.

ABOVE The British public and press embraced the energetic, photogenic Kennedys. The *Times* of London opined, "[Joe Sr.'s] appointment would have caused quite a stir some years ago, when the Irish question was an obstacle to better Anglo-American relations. Now it will provoke little more than wonder that it has not occurred before."

The low point of appeasement came in the summer and fall of 1939 with the Munich crisis. Since taking power in 1933, Adolph Hitler had re-armed Germany in defiance of the Versailles Treaty, and he was bent on bringing all ethnic Germans under one flag and empire—the Nazi reich. In 1938, Hitler annexed Austria, essentially grafting all of Austria onto Germany proper. Now, Hitler demanded that Czechoslovakia give Germany its western provinces—the Sudetenland—which were mostly populated by ethnic Germans.

For weeks it seemed as if war was imminent. In late September, Prime Minister Neville Chamberlain flew to Munich to meet with Hitler. He returned with an agreement that he said would bring "peace in our time." Germany got the Sudetenland. In return, the democracies got a promise that Hitler would leave the rest of the country alone. Joe Sr. vocally and publicly supported the deal. Six months later, German forces occupied the remainder of Czechoslovakia.

Jack had a front-row seat for these events. Along with Joe Jr., Jack spent the summer of 1938 working at the embassy in London, and he planned on spending much of 1939 not at Harvard but based in London, gathering material on the senior thesis he intended to write for the newly established Harvard School of Government. At Harvard, he'd sailed for the Harvard Yacht Club and rejoiced in his acceptance into Spee, one of the university's exclusive "final clubs." But his 1937 road trip with Billings had stirred Jack's restless curiosity about current events. He was more serious now. Big things were happening in the world, and he wanted to understand them.

Meanwhile, his father was becoming ever more shrill in his contention that war was coming and that Britain would lose. He cited reports by the famous aviator Charles Lindbergh, who toured German air bases and aircraft factories and sent back wildly inflated production statistics (supplied by the Germans) of German armament.

In March 1939, Joe Sr. sent Jack on a long solo trip that took in Poland, the Baltic states, Russia, Romania, Turkey, Egypt, and Palestine. That summer, there was one more European road trip, in the last days of uneasy peace. On this trip, Jack took along his Harvard roommate, Torbert Macdonald. Speeding through France, Jack managed to flip their car. Upside-down, Jack turned to "Torby" and said, "Well, pal, we didn't make it, did we?"

On the first of September, having struck a deal with Soviet dictator Josef Stalin, Hitler invaded. Two days later, Jack joined his parents, Joe Jr., and Kick in the Strangers Gallery of the House of Commons to hear Neville Chamberlain declare that Britain was at war with Germany for the second time in twenty-five years. Afterward, Joe Sr. made a transatlantic phone call to FDR. "It's the end of the world," he told the president. "The end of everything."

That very night, a German submarine sank the British passenger liner *Athenia* off the Irish coast. More than one hundred people died, including twenty-eight Americans. Joe Sr. dispatched Jack to Glasgow, Scotland, where the survivors were being kept, to assure the American passengers that the embassy would secure their passage to the United States as quickly as possible. Understandably frightened, the Americans said that they wouldn't board any homeward ship unless it had a naval escort. Jack tried unsuccessfully to persuade them that they'd be safe on any ship flying the flag of the neutral

ATHENIA SURVIVORS DEMAND U.S. NAVY CONVOY

WOMEN APPEAL TO AMBASSADOR'S SON

FROM OUR SPECIAL CORRESPONDENT

GLASGOW, Thursday.

Mr. John Kennedy, the 18-year-old son of the United States Ambassador, faced a determined audience of fellow Americans who had survived the torpedoing of the British liner Athenia in the lounge of an hotel here this afternoon, and heard their polite but firm demands for some assurance of adequate protection when, next week, they sail for home in a specially chartered freighter now on its way from New York.

This schoolboy diplomat had been sent overnight to Glasgow to tell the Athenia survivors what their Government is doing to alleviate their distress and get them home.

"I talked to my father this morning, and he has spoken to America since," he said. "He asked me to tell you that the Government has plenty of money for you all.

ENGLISH AND CANADIANS

"Ten thousand dollars (£2,000) has been allocated for your immediate wants, ocean tickets will be provided and a ship is on the way. We do not know where she is going to dock, but you will all be gathered together and return in the same ship.

"The Consul-General here will tell you when you go and where from. It should be some time next week. Although it is primarily for United States citizens, if any English people or Canadians are with a particular party we shall endeavour to accommodate them."

He then invited questions and, answering one woman, said the ship would be here in seven days' time and leave immediately. Although it was a small ship there was plenty of room, and there would be more room than if they tried to squeeze them aboard an already too crowded liner.

When Mr. Kennedy said that it was much better to be in an American boat than a British one in a convoy there were many interruptions.

"WHAT ABOUT MINES?"

"What about danger from mines?" said one woman. "We must have a convoy," cried another. "You can't trust the German navy, anyway," said a man.

Mr. Kennedy explained that President Roosevelt had said that there was no need for a convoy, as American ships would not be attacked.

"You cannot trust the Germans. They fired on us," retorted one woman.

Another man said: "Twenty grand new cruisers and many destroyers are just in commission. The United States Government can spare a few of them. Women who have been through what these have in the last few days will not feel safe without protection.

"One flier came down in the ocean a little while ago. They sent out the whole Pacific Fleet from America to find him."

Young Mr. Kennedy looked tense as he replied: "I will tell my father all you say. I know he will consider all aspects."

The meeting ended with two minutes' silence for the dead on the suggestion of the Consul-General, Mr. Leslie Davis.

After the meeting Mr. Kennedy went among the audience answering their personal problems. He had spent the morning at local hospitals visiting those whose injuries necessitated detention, and then lunched with the Lord Provost of Glasgow.

Before lunch he told me it was calculated there were still 8,000 Americans in Britain who wanted to go home and that freighters were being sent so that all should be evacuated before Oct. 1.

I asked about himself and his brothers and sisters. "Oh," he replied, "we must get back to school, but we shan't go until all other American citizens have gone."

Miss Sirine, chaperon to a party of girl students, who spent many hours in the water and at least one of whom is missing, said to me: "We are not leaving this country unless we are given adequate protection, whether the United States is neutral or not." A number of women standing near echoed her remark.

Realising the heavy strain on the accommodation that Galway can offer, Glasgow has invited all the Athenia survivors who were landed at the Eire port to come here, and hotels are preparing to receive about 400. Those fit to travel are expected to arrive to-morrow morning.

New figures are given to-day by the shipping company, who say that 560 survivors landed in Glasgow, 510 in Galway; 220 are on the City of Flint. The ship's complement is now given as 1,418, of which 315 were crew.

United States. The meeting broke up acrimoniously, but Jack kept his composure. It was his first time acting in an official capacity for the U.S. government.

Shortly afterward, Jack made his first transatlantic flight aboard a Pan American Clipper flying boat (the first regular transatlantic airplane service) to start his senior year at Harvard. Back in Cambridge, there was the usual social round, and Jack was thrilled to be named to the business board of Harvard's newspaper, the *Crimson*. He still struggled with his stomach; switching from a milk-based diet to one consisting mostly of starches didn't seem to help.

Despite ongoing stomach problems, Jack worked with relentless energy on his senior honors thesis, to be titled "Appeasement at Munich." His research focused on the British government's appeasement

LEFT A newspaper story printed on September 8, 1939, relating Jack's encounter with the American survivors of the torpedoed liner *Athenia.* ABOVE A Kennedy vacation snapshot taken in France during the summer of 1939, the start of World War II just weeks away.

REPORT ON THESIS FOR DISTINCTION

Name of Candidate ....KENNEDY, J.F. '40...

Title of Thesis ....APPEASEMENT AT MUNICH..

....

Grade *Magna cum laude*..

(Indicate whether rank is *summa cum laude*, *magna cum laude*, or *cum laude*, or not
of distinction grade (C, D or E). Use *plus* or *minus*, where necessary.)

Remarks (Please indicate more fully the special excellences or defects of the thesis.)

Badly written; but a laborious, interesting and intelligent discussion of a difficult question.

Henry A. Yeomans (Signature)

policies of the 1930s. He was tackling a big subject. Most of his classmates at the School of Government

chose less contentious topics, such as the McNary-Haugen Farm Relief Bill, but Jack's was a subject for

which his experiences had prepared him well. And with a diplomat father, he had resources the average

undergraduate could only dream of. He thought nothing of firing off a cablegram to James Seymour,

his father's press secretary in London, asking Seymour to track down and send some obscure report or

policy paper. At one point, Seymour wired back, "Dear Jack, your cables get tougher." In order to com-

plete his thesis, Jack spent so much time in the library that his friends joked, "How's the book coming,

Jack?" The end result was as long as a book—about 30,000 words.

In the end, "Appeasement at Munich" was a vague defense of the policy of appeasement on

the grounds that it bought time for Britain to build up its defenses, especially in the air. The paper

was also critical of Neville Chamberlain. Apparently, Jack didn't realize—despite all his research—

that Chamberlain had staunchly supported re-armament throughout the period. A board of

four professors reviewed the thesis. Their comments ranged from "badly written" to "fundamental

premise not analyzed" to "interesting and intelligent" and "[a work showing] real interest and a

reasonable amount of work." In the end, it won the accolade *magna cum laude*. In truth, it was far

from a polished effort, and sometimes just what Jack was getting at wasn't exactly clear. As Joe Jr.

ABOVE Professor Henry Yeomans's report on "Appeasement at Munich." While Jack's *magna cum laude*
wasn't the highest possible grade, it was higher than the *cum laude* Joe Jr. earned for his senior thesis.
RIGHT Farewell to Harvard Yard: A cap-and-gowned Jack at his graduation.

remarked to Joe Sr. after reading the thesis, "It seems to represent a lot of work, but it does not prove anything."

Nevertheless, Jack showed the thesis to Arthur Krock, a family friend and Pulitzer Prize–winning *New York Times* journalist who'd ghostwritten a pro-Roosevelt book published by Joe Sr. during the presidential campaign of 1936. Krock was convinced that Jack's paper could indeed be a book for commercial publication. From London, Joe Sr. jumped on the idea. Krock edited "Appeasement at Munich" into publishable form and suggested a new title, *Why England Slept*—a conscious answer to *While England Slept*, Winston Churchill's attack on appeasement published in 1938. When major publishing houses declined to publish the manuscript, Krock's literary agent found a home for it with a smaller house, and Joe Sr. persuaded Henry Luce, influential publisher of *Time* and *Life* magazines, to write the foreword.

Why England Slept hit bookstores in the late summer of 1940 and sold modestly well. Rumors circulated that the book's success was owed to Joe Sr. personally buying up thousands of copies. He may have done something like that, but the book most likely succeeded because it was highly topical, appearing at a point where Americans were struggling to make sense of the conflict in Europe and how the country should respond to it.

There were some who noted that in the broadest sense, *Why England Slept* reflected Joe Sr.'s views, and in some quarters the book was regarded as little more than Jack's defense of his father. One of Jack's former professors joked that it should have been titled *While Daddy Slept*.

Such carping aside, the book's success must have gratified Jack. Despite the help of Krock and the influence of Joe Sr., this was *his* achievement, one he didn't have to share with anyone—including his older brother.

Jack donated the profits from the British edition of *Why England Slept* to a fund to help English victims of German air raids. With the profits from the U.S. edition, Jack bought himself a graduation present, a brand-new, bright-green Buick convertible.

He had now passed out of Harvard Yard. Where to next?

Enclosures

LETTER Jack sent his thesis to Joe Sr. in London by diplomatic pouch rather than conventional mail because he presumed "all letters [to the ambassador] are read" by the British intelligence services. **THESIS DRAFT** An excerpt from the final draft of the "Appeasement at Munich," which would become *Why England Slept*. Jack told Joe Sr. that the thesis represented "more work than I've ever done in my life."

RIGHT A snapshot of young Jack with a published copy of his book, *Why England Slept*.

FROM *the* SOUTH PACIFIC *to the* SENATE

2.

JOHN FITZGERALD KENNEDY
Born May 29, 1917, in Brookline, Massachusetts. Prepared at The Choate School. Home Address: 294 Pondfield Road, Bronxville, New York. Winthrop House. *Crimson* (2–4); Chairman Smoker Committee (1); St. Paul's Catholic Club (1–4). Football (1), Junior Varsity (2); Swimming (1), Squad (2). Golf (1). House Hockey (3, 4); House Swimming (2); House Softball (4). Hasty Pudding-Institute of 1770; Spee Club. Permanent Class Committee. Field of Concentration: Government. Intended Vocation: Law.

DESPITE JACK'S DREAMS of a career in teaching or writing, he'd put down "law" as his intended vocation in his Harvard yearbook, and he'd told friends that he planned to enter Yale Law School in fall 1941. In the meantime, Jack decided to head west to Stanford University in Palo Alto, California, to take some courses in business law.

Arriving in September 1940, Jack found himself already a big man on campus as the author of *Why England Slept* and the son of Ambassador Kennedy. "Photographers were always taking his picture," recalled a woman who had dated Jack at the time. "He was sort of a mini-celebrity."

The climate and the co-eds in California appealed to Jack. "Have become quite fond of Stanford," he wrote to Lem Billings. "Everyone is very friendly—the gals are quite attractive—and it's a very good life." On weekends, there were jaunts down the coast to Hollywood, where his Kennedy name won him access to exclusive nightclubs and A-list parties. Here he met stars like Clark Gable and Lana Turner.

In the same month Jack arrived at Stanford, Congress passed—by one vote—the Selective Service Act, establishing the first peacetime military draft in U.S. history. Along with millions of American men between ages twenty-one and thirty-five, Jack lined up to register on October 18. Three weeks later, literally by the luck of the draw, Jack became one of the first men called up by the Army, although he wouldn't have to report for his physical until the end of the academic year in July 1941.

The prospect of that physical exam scared Jack. He knew that given his medical history, he had little chance of passing. "They will never take me in the Army," he wrote to Lem Billings, "and yet if I don't go, it will look quite bad," certainly referencing his father's growing notoriety.

LEFT The official U.S. Navy portrait of Jack, wearing the insignia of a lieutenant, junior grade on his uniform.

ABOVE Jack's 1940 Harvard yearbook entry, in which he listed "law" as his intended vocation.

don't like it at all. After all, it remained for
London to receive the worst bombing since Rotterdam
and remember that this city is attempting to
function while all this is going on, whereas Warsaw
and Rotterdam were evacuated.

I am feeling very well. Haven't the slightest
touch of nervousness. But I can see evidences of
some people beginning to break down. Herschel
Johnson was almost killed Sunday night when the house
next door to him was blown right off the map. The
Natural History Museum in Kensington was practically
gutted by bombs and fire Sunday night, so all in all
Jack, it is a great experience. The only thing I am
afraid of is that I won't be able to live long enough
to tell all that I see and feel about this crisis.
When I hear these mental midgets talking about my ~ U.S.A.
desire for appeasement and being critical of it, my
blood fairly boils. What is this war going to prove?
And what is it going to do to civilization? The answer
to the first question is nothing; and to the second
I shudder even to think about it.

The second air raid warning is going off while
I am dictating this to you at 4 o'clock in the afternoon, but until it gets really tough I am carrying on.

Good luck to you Boy, and I hope to see you soon.

Love,
Dad.

My last passport was obtained from ___Washington___ on ___May___, ___1938___
(Insert Washington or location of office abroad)   (Date)

Dip. 1876 — June 14, 1938

and is submitted herewith for cancelation ___This Passport was taken up in October, 1939, when___
(Give disposition of passport if it cannot be submitted)
___I returned to U. S.___

Returned

I intend to visit the following countries for the purposes indicated:

___Brazil, Argentina, Chile___   ___Study___
(Names of countries to be visited)   (Purposes of visits)

and I intend to return to the United States within ___two___ { months.
~~years~~

ADDRESS

I request that my passport be mailed to the following address:

[NOTE.—A passport will not be mailed to a hotel address unless the hotel is the applicant's place of permanent residence.]

Name ___John F. Kennedy___   *OK*

Number and street ___℅ Paul Murphy___

___Somerset Importers, 9 Rockefeller Plaza,___

City and State ___New York City, New York,___

DESCRIPTION AND PHOTOGRAPH OF APPLICANT

Height ___6___ feet, ___0___ inches.

Hair ___bblonde___

Eyes ___b lue___

Distinguishing marks or features _____
(Note any marks or scars on hands or face)

___none___
by which applicant may be identified)

Place of birth ___Brookline, Mass.___
(City and State)

Date of birth ___May 29, 1917___
(Month, day, and year)

Occupation ___Student___

I solemnly swear that the statements made on both sides of this application are true and that the photograph attached hereto is a likeness of me.

OATH OF ALLEGIANCE

Further, I do solemnly swear that I will support and defend the Constitution of the United States against all enemies, foreign and domestic; that I will bear true faith and allegiance to the same; and that I take this obligation freely, without any mental reservation, or purpose of evasion: So help me God.

John Fitzgerald Kennedy
(Signature of applicant)

Subscribed and sworn to before me this ___16th___ day of ___April___, 19__41__

[SEAL OF COURT]   ___J. ALEX ARNETTE___

Clerk of the ___Circuit___ Court at ___West Palm Beach, Fla.,___

By *Merle P. Johnston*   D. C.

AFFIDAVIT OF IDENTIFYING WITNESS

I, the undersigned, solemnly swear that I am a citizen of the United States; that I reside at the address written below my signature hereto affixed; that I know the applicant who executed the affidavit hereinbefore set forth to be a citizen of the United States; that the statements made in the applicant's affidavit are true to the best of my knowledge and belief; further, I solemnly swear that I have known the applicant personally for _____ years.

If witness has been issued a passport, give number if known and date or approximate date of issue.

No. ___--___ Date of issue ___--___

No lawyer or other person will be accepted as witness to a passport application if he has received or expects to receive a fee for his services or in connection with the execution of the application or obtaining the passport.

___An Old passport heretofore submitted___
___in lieu of identifying witness.___
(Signature of witness)

_____
(Residence address of witness)

Subscribed and sworn to before me this _____ day of _____, 19____

Already scorned by the British public as a defeatist, some now accused Joe Sr. of being too quick to run for air-raid shelters when German bombers began their "blitz" of London. Shortly after FDR won reelection for an unprecedented third term in November, Joe Sr. gave an interview to several journalists. Under the mistaken impression he was speaking off the record, he declared, "Democracy is finished in England . . . it may be here [in the United States]," with some anti-Semitic comments thrown in.

> LEFT Joe Sr. described the German air raids in this excerpt from a letter to Jack from London, noting that "this city is attempting to function," and that he personally didn't have "the slightest touch of nervousness."
> ABOVE Documentation for Jack's passage to South America in 1941, after which he quickly enlisted in the Navy.

When his words hit print, it was clear in Washington and Whitehall that Joe Sr. finally had to go. Choosing to jump rather than be pushed, he resigned and headed home. The interview killed whatever remaining political ambitions Joe Sr. had for himself.

While Jack saw his entrance into the military as essential, his big brother Joe Jr. was also taking the first steps toward a political career. He'd begun to gain nationwide attention for publishing an article in the *Atlantic Monthly* magazine, serving as a delegate to the 1940 Democratic National Convention, and generally becoming known as a leading figure among the younger breed of isolationists. In June 1941, Jack returned home from a trip to South America to find that his brother had beaten him into uniform by enlisting in the U.S. Navy Reserve.

Jack quickly applied to the Army's Officer Candidate School—and flunked the physical. He also failed the physical for the Navy. So Joe Sr. leaned on Rear Admiral Roland Kirk, formerly his naval attaché in London, to have the Board of Medical Review give Jack another chance. Kirk, in turn, leaned on the doctors to make sure that Jack passed this time. In the resulting exam, the board noted that Jack had had "the usual childhood diseases" and had once been on a "restricted diet," but his only medical defect was three missing teeth. Shortly afterward, John F. Kennedy became Ensign John F. Kennedy, USNR.

THE INGA BINGA AFFAIR

October 1941 found Ensign Kennedy at a basement desk at the Office of Naval Intelligence (ONI) writing up "Foreign Intelligence Assessments." It wasn't a very challenging job, and it left him free to take part in the capital's social life in the evenings, often in the company of his sister Kick, who was working for the *Times-Herald* newspaper. It was through Kick that he met Inga Arvad.

A stunningly beautiful, blue-eyed blond of Danish birth, twenty-eight-year-old Arvad had already lived a remarkable life. She'd married and divorced an Egyptian diplomat while still in her teens, then married a Hungarian-American filmmaker, Paul Fejos, hoping to parlay that liaison into a movie career. While a movie career didn't work out, Arvad quickly learned that by lying about her journalistic credentials and exploiting personal connections, she could score interviews with Germany's Nazi bigwigs. She was even able to arrange for two meetings with Hitler himself. When Fejos went to South America to search for ancient ruins in 1940, Arvad moved to New York City to take journalism classes at Columbia University.

At Columbia, she met Arthur Krock. Dazzled by her looks, if not her reportage, he recommended Arvad for a job at the *Times-Herald*, where she wrote a column profiling "interesting" Washingtonians. Among her subjects was Jack, whom she described as "a boy with a future." Sometime in November, Jack and Inga—whom he dubbed "Inga Binga"— became lovers.

RIGHT Jack's lover Inga Arvad's good looks and charm masked a fiercely ambitious and viciously anti-Semitic personality. Here she poses as Miss Denmark in 1931.

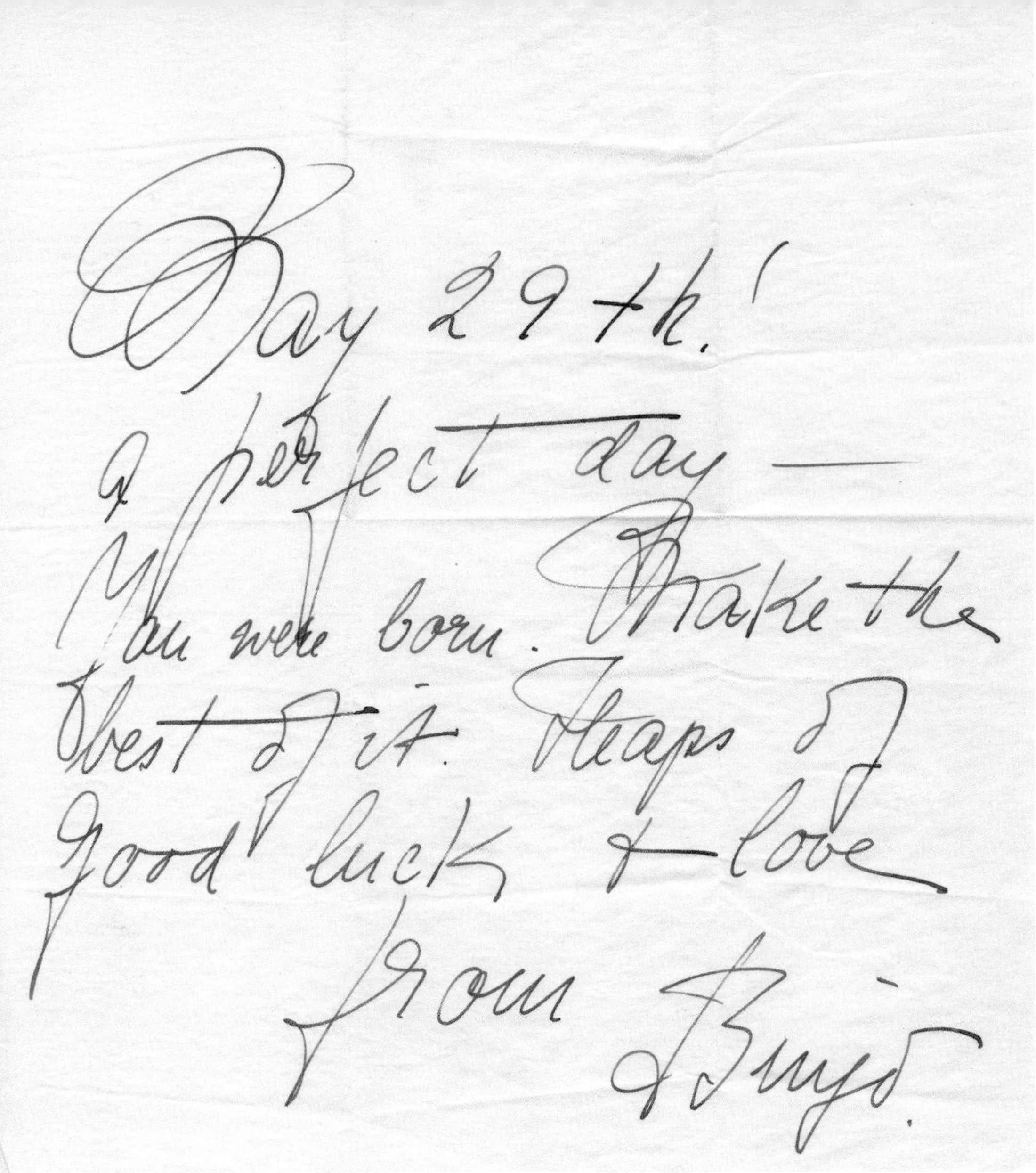

May 29th!
a perfect day —
You were born. Make the
best of it. Heaps of
good luck & love
from
Binga.

Like most Americans, Jack had focused on events in Europe during the first years of war. Events on the other side of the world, however, finally brought the United States into the conflict. Pressured by the Roosevelt administration over its war in China, Japan launched a devastating attack on the U.S. Naval Base at Pearl Harbor, Hawaii, on December 7, 1941. Japan was allied to Germany and Italy, and those nations declared war on the United States a few days later.

Enclosures

NAVY IDENTIFICATION CARD "To any man who may be asked in this century what he did to make his life worthwhile," Jack wrote as president, "I think can respond with a good deal of pride and satisfaction, 'I served in the United States Navy.'" MEDICAL FILE Jack's Navy physical exam, which biographer Robert Dallek called "a complete whitewash."

ABOVE A birthday note to Jack "from Binga." Jack found not only physical gratification but also emotional support and intellectual rapport with the Danish beauty. RIGHT Jack, resplendent in dress white uniform, greets a visitor to the Sixth Naval District's base in Charleston.

NMS Form Y
(1939)

REPORT OF PHYSICAL EXAMINATION

Purpose of this examination ____ Appt. as I-V(S), USNR. ____

Place of duty ____ Place of examination ____ Date of exam ____

Name **KENNEDY, John Fitzgerald**
(Surname first, Christian names in full)

Rank **Candidate** Date of birth ____

Place of birth ____ **Mass.**

Family history ____ **Negative** ____

History of illness or injury ____ Usual childhood diseases. Tsd 1935. Appendec

restricted as regular diet to no fried foods or roughage. No ul

Head and face ____ **Normal**

Eyes: Pupils (size, shape, reaction to light and distance, etc.) ____ **Normal**

Distant vision Rt. ____ 20 ____ /20, corrected to ____ /20 by ____

Lt. ____ 20 ____ /20, corrected to ____ /20 by ____

Color perception ____ **Normal**

Binocular vision ____
(Without lenses—Recorded only when visual defects exist) ____ (State edition of Stilling's plates used)

Disease or anatomical defects ____ **None**

Ears: Hearing Rt. Watch ____ /40'' Coin click ____ /20' Whispered voice ____ /15' Spoken voice ____ /15'
Lt. Watch ____ /40'' Coin click ____ /20' Whispered voice ____ 15' Spoken voice ____ /15'

Binaural ____ /15'. Disease or defects ____ **None**
(Spoken voice)

Nose ____ **Normal**
(Disease or anatomical defect, obstruction, etc. State degree)

UNITED STATES NAVY
Identification Card

KENNEDY, John F.
Name

John F. Kennedy
Signature

Color Hair **Brown** Eyes **Green**
Weight **150** Birth **5-29-17**
Void after **D.O.W.**

LIEUT. USNR

N. Nav. 546 ____ Validating Officer

Sinuses _____

Tongue, palate, pharynx, larynx, tonsils _____ Normal

Teeth and gums (disease or anatomical defect): _____ Normal

Missing teeth __1, 17, 32.__ _____ None
    (List numbers)

Nonvital teeth _____ None
    (List numbers)

Periapical disease _____ None
    (List numbers)

Marked malocclusion _____ No
    (Degree)

Lack of serviceable occlusion _____ No
    (Yes or no)

Pyorrhea alveolaris _____ None
    (Degree)

Teeth replaced by bridges _____ None
    (List numbers)

Meets dental requirements _____ YES

Dentures _____ None
    (Yes or no)

General build and appearance _____ Slender
    (Description)

Temperature __98.4__ Chest at expiration __34__
    (State whether slender, medium, or heavy, and required abnormalities)

Height __71½__ Chest at inspiration __36__

Weight __155__ Circumference of abdomen at umbilicus __27__

Neck (abnormalities, thyroid gland, trachea, larynx) __Normal__

Skin, hair, and glands __Normal__

Recent gain or loss, amount and cause __None__

Spine and extremities (bones, joints, muscles, feet) __Normal__

Mark missing teeth by X whether replaced or not. Show size and position of caries in black, use red to indicate fillings and restorations.

RIGHT   2 3 4 5 6 7 8 9 10 11 12 13 14 15 16

18 19 20 21 22 23 24 25 26 27 28 29 30 31 32   LEFT

S. LITTIG, Lt-Comdr., DC-V(S), USNR.
(Signature of dental examiner)

Ensign Kennedy now found himself working long overnight shifts at the ONI, though he still made time for Arvad. Coincidentally, another female reporter at the *Times-Herald*—a rival for Jack's affections—reported Arvad to the FBI as a possible Nazi spy. Arvad boldly demanded that FBI director J. Edgar Hoover personally clear her name.

Arvad might not have been so bold had she known that she was already under investigation by the FBI. One of her fellow Columbia students had denounced her on the basis of anti-Semitic and pro-Nazi statements. Hoover had taken a personal interest in the case, ordering Arvad's phone tapped and her mail intercepted and read. The surveillance revealed that Arvad was indeed a hater of Jews and an admirer of Herr Hitler, but that she had no connections to the regime itself.

Hoover informed the Chief of Naval Operations, Admiral Ernest J. King, that this beautiful Nazi sympathizer was having an affair with a naval intelligence officer. Even though he was a low-ranking officer without a high-security clearance, the situation was dubious and retribution was swift. On January 13, 1942, the Navy sent Jack to the weeds with a transfer to a base at Charleston, South Carolina.

By then, news of the affair had hit the press, thanks to Walter Winchell, a hugely influential gossip columnist, in the *New York Mirror* newspaper: "One of Ex-Ambassador Kennedy's eligible sons is

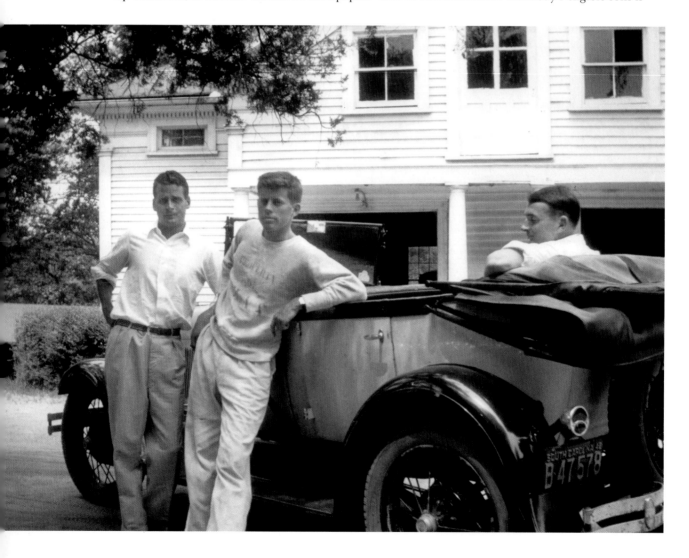

ABOVE Jack relaxes off-duty at the Office of Naval Intelligence's field office in Charleston, South Carolina, 1942.
RIGHT Jack's uniform bears the single stripe and star of an ensign in this photograph taken during his stint in Charleston. In October 1942, he won promotion to lieutenant, junior grade.

the target of a Washington gal columnist's affections. So much so that she has consulted her barrister about divorcing her exploring groom. Pa Kennedy no like." Indeed. For a while, Jack tried to keep up a long-distance relationship with Arvad, but they broke up in February—by which time, Arvad was already seeing another man.

The Winchell column was likely the first, and one of the few times ever, that Jack's pre- and extramarital affairs surfaced in the press. In the 1940s–60s, the press was deferential to the rich, the powerful, and the famous. As his career advanced, Kennedy went out of his way to cultivate relationships with journalists and to charm the press.

It is impossible to tell the full story of Kennedy's life without addressing his sexual dalliances and exploits. According to Lem Billings, he and Jack lost their virginity in a New York City brothel in 1934, when Jack would have been seventeen. He usually had a steady girlfriend (or two) during his prep school and college years, and he proposed marriage to at least one young woman (Anne Cannon, heiress to a textile fortune) and possibly others. But being in a relationship never stopped him from pursuing pleasure elsewhere.

Through his wide-ranging reading, Jack had come to admire the lives of the eighteenth- and nineteenth-century English aristocrats who'd managed to combine public service with promiscuity. Certainly, an even greater influence on Jack's attitude toward women was his father. He absorbed his father's conviction that rules were meant to be broken (as a boy, he must have figured out what was going on when Joe returned from long absences bearing lavish gifts for Rose), and that everything in life was a competition. Jack thrived on risk. Whether behind the wheel of a car (he was a notoriously reckless driver) or the tiller of a sailboat, on the football field or in pursuit of women, he never did things by halves.

This love of risk probably explains why he was willing to continue his philandering even after becoming a married man, a U.S. senator, and ultimately president, knowing that—despite an utterly loyal staff and a mostly compliant press—exposure of his infidelities could wreck everything he'd achieved. During his affair with Washington socialite Mary Pinchot Meyer, for example, he once escorted her to a White House elevator after an assignation, leaving her with a grin and the admonition to "look virginal" for the Secret Service.

Jack bedded hundreds of women in his lifetime. His conquests included actresses Ava Gardner, Gene Tierney, and Marilyn Monroe, politician and journalist Clare Booth Luce, the above-mentioned Mary Pinchot Meyer, and (in the words of one of his biographers) countless "coeds, models, showgirls, and starlets," not to mention strippers, stewardesses, and various "secretaries," including a pair nicknamed "fiddle and faddle" whose main duties were to provide companionship during his nude swims in the White House pool.

Jack's sex life was marked more by quantity than quality, and his liaisons were usually brief. He reportedly described his own technique as "slam, bam, thank you, ma'am." And by all accounts, he was

a self-absorbed lover. "We have only fifteen minutes," he told one woman. Another caught him looking

at his watch during sex. Inga Arvad said he was "[a]wkward and groping. A boy, not a man. Intent

upon [satisfying himself] and not a woman's pleasure." Another conquest more charitably noted that

Jack was "[n]ice . . . considerate in his own way, witty and fun. But he gave off light instead of heat. Sex

was something to have done, not to be doing. He wasn't in it for the cuddling."

Jack probably would have agreed. He once reportedly told a friend, "I'm not interested in car-

rying on . . . I like the conquest. That's the challenge. I like the contest between male and female—

that's what I like. It's the chase I like—not the kill!" It was a "contest" that Jack believed he needed to

engage in often. At a meeting with British Prime Minister Harold Macmillan in 1961, Jack shocked the

premier by asking, "I wonder how it is with you, Harold? If I don't have a woman for three days, I get

terrible headaches."

ABOVE A tanned, bare-chested Lieutenant Kennedy on the bridge of PT-109 at the Tulagi base in the
Solomon Islands.

THE SAGA OF PT-109

In the spring of 1942, Kennedy continued to command a desk in Charleston. Determined to do more than just push paper, he pressed continually for sea duty. The United States was now engaged in a war with Japan that stretched across the South Pacific, and Kennedy wanted a piece of the action. In July, he was appointed to Midshipman's school in Illinois. There, Kennedy and his fellow students were briefed on the Navy's new PT-boat program by Lieutenant Commander John Bulkeley.

PT ("Patrol Torpedo") boats were plywood crafts about eighty feet long. Their three 12-cylinder engines gave them a top speed of about fifty miles an hour, and they carried four torpedo tubes and four .50-caliber machine guns. The idea was that the PTs would slip out of their bases at night to attack Japanese supply ships, troop transports, and their destroyer escorts.

LEFT Jack in the Solomon Islands. One PT crewman later told a historian, "Well, he was a young, lanky officer, bright, active, highly idealist . . . always concerned about the welfare of his crew, this was one of his outstanding traits." ABOVE Jack (far right) and crew aboard PT-109 in 1943. Like most PT boats, the 109's usual complement was an officer and nine enlisted men; Jack had a couple of extra men aboard the night the boat was rammed and sunk.

Kennedy was determined to become a PT-boat skipper. The odds were long: The ratio of applicants to open spots was 1,024 to 50, exactly. True to form, Joe Sr. stepped in, taking Bulkeley to lunch to make a pitch for his son, but also appealing to the officer not to send his son anywhere "too deadly." Bulkeley approved Jack's assignment to PT training school.

In training in Rhode Island, Lieutenant Kennedy did well—so well that he was made an instructor. But his ambitions reached beyond teaching; he wanted to be where the action was. He appealed to Massachusetts Senator David Walsh, who had Navy connections, to be assigned to a post abroad. On March 6, 1943, Kennedy sailed from San Francisco for the Solomon Islands. U.S. forces had finally driven the Japanese from the strategically vital island of Guadalcanal, one of the Solomon Islands, after months of bitter fighting on land, at sea, and in the air.

On April 7, as Kennedy's troop ship approached Guadalcanal, the convoy came under attack by Japanese warplanes. A destroyer nearby took a direct hit and sank. Another bomb exploded so close to Kennedy's ship that the concussion snapped the captain's neck, killing him instantly, and buckled the ship's bow. Every gun in the small fleet blazed away at the sky. Kennedy calmly passed ammunition to the crew of a 40 mm antiaircraft gun. Even before reaching his squadron's base at Tulagi, Kennedy had proved that he could endure the crucible of combat with calm and composure. At the end of the action, Kennedy watched as a downed Japanese pilot parachuted into the sea and then drew a pistol when the ship's crew tried to pick him up. A sailor standing near Jack shot the flier with a rifle and "took the top of his head off," Jack wrote to Joe Sr. and Rose.

Once in the combat zone, Jack wrote Inga, "A number of my illusions have been shattered." He was far too intelligent and worldly to have any real illusions about the nature of war, but what he experienced now shocked him. He was particularly surprised by the incompetence and indifference of many of the "top brass," whom he denounced in scathing but funny letters home: "Even the simple delivery of a letter frequently overburdens this heaving puffing war machine of ours. God save this country of ours from those patriots whose war cry is 'what this country needs is to be run with military efficiency.'"

Kennedy was particularly appalled by the morale of the men who'd been in the islands for many months, enduring withering heat and humidity, insects, tropical diseases, boredom, bad and monotonous food, and the terror of Japanese air raids. They continued to do their jobs, but they desperately wanted to go home. This attitude contrasted sharply with the rah-rah patriotism shown by those safely stateside. Kennedy wrote, "It's one of the interesting things about this war that everyone in the States . . . wants to be out here killing Japs, while everyone here wants to back at the Stork Club [a famous New York night spot]. It seems to me that someone with enterprise could work out some sort of exchange."

In late April, Lieutenant Kennedy got his first command: PT-109. Popular with officers and enlisted men alike, he had no trouble in assembling a crew. "I thought he was a real good officer," one of his sailors recalled. "His boat was shipshape and his crew was well organized, orderly . . . he was

RIGHT Jack leaning on a cane amidst the lush tropical foliage of the Solomon Islands, 1943.

a fellow who made you feel good to be with—and you would never have known about his personal, privileged life by visiting with him . . . He was always a genuine person."

At night, Jack took PT-109 out on training patrols. During the day, he holed up in a hut on shore, stretched out on a Navy mattress reinforced with a board to ease his back pain, reading and writing sardonic letters. A friend he'd made during PT training in Rhode Island, Paul "Red" Fay, tried to teach him poker. Unlike many of the men who ultimately moved into the White House, however, Jack never developed an interest in the game.

With the Solomons secured, Jack's squadron moved north, first to the Russell Islands, and then to Rendova, near New Georgia Island. On the pitch-black night of August 1—the longest night of the year—PT-109 and its twelve-man crew joined up with fourteen other PT boats and headed into Blackett

ABOVE Jack (second from left) with three fellow officers (left to right): Jim Reed, George Ross, and Paul Fay. After the war "Red" Fay became a close political adviser and was eventually appointed undersecretary of the Navy.

Strait. Their objective: to intercept the "Tokyo Express," destroyers taking troops and supplies from the big Japanese base at Rabaul to reinforce the garrison on Kolombangara Island.

It was the biggest PT-boat operation so far in the war, and it was a dismal failure. The torpedoes issued to PTs were old and practically all duds. The wake that the boats threw up meant that Japanese ships or planes could easily spot them before they could attack. And the combination of wooden hulls and tanks full of high-octane fuel could turn a PT into a fireball if hit. Only four of the fifteen PTs in the operation had radar, so when the PTs made contact with four Japanese destroyers, the result was a confused melee—Japanese floatplanes dropping flares, American PTs firing torpedoes that hit nothing—while the Tokyo Express slipped past, landed their troops and supplies, and headed back up the strait.

By then, all but three of the PTs in the area—109 being one of them—had withdrawn. At around 2:00 a.m. on August 2, a shape loomed out of the darkness. Kennedy hoped it was another PT. But it was the Japanese destroyer *Amagari*. Kennedy frantically spun the wheel, hoping to make a torpedo attack, but he was too late. The *Amagari* sliced PT-109 in half. Two sailors died in the collision. The skipper and the surviving crew went into the water. Spilled fuel ignited and Master Machinist Mate Pat McMahon suffered severe burns before the *Amagari*'s wake dispersed the flaming water. Kennedy rounded up his men in the water and had them cling to PT-109's wreckage.

They floated until early afternoon on August 2, when what was left of PT-109 began to sink. As they were in enemy-controlled waters, with Japanese bases on the surrounding islands, their only hope of surviving and avoiding capture was to swim to some small islands to the East.

Nine of the crew clung to a floating plank as they paddled to land. Kennedy took the straps of his wounded man, McMahon's, lifejacket between his teeth and towed him the whole way. This act of incredible endurance was even more astonishing, given the state of Kennedy's back.

Four hours later, the men staggered ashore on a tiny speck of land known as Plum Pudding Island. Despite his pain and exhaustion, Kennedy insisted on swimming far out to sea after darkness fell, hoping to signal any passing PT boats. None came.

The men couldn't stay on Plum Pudding Island; it was too exposed, and there was no water apart from a few mouthfuls of rainwater the survivors managed to lick from leaves or catch with their own mouths. So on August 4, Kennedy ordered his men into the water again. This time the destination was Olsana Island, where there were coconut palms.

The next day, while the remainder of the crew rested on Olsana, Kennedy and Ensign Barney Ross swam to nearby Nauru Island. Here, they spotted two Melanesian islanders in a canoe. Fearing that the American soldiers were Japanese, the islanders paddled away. Kennedy and Ross were able to find some candy and a can of water on Nauru, but this was far from the help they needed.

When Jack swam back to Olsana on August 6 (Ross remained on Naru to rest) he found the two islanders mingling with PT-109's elated survivors. The islanders, two men named Biuku and Eroni, worked for Lieutenant Arthur Evans of the Royal Austrian Navy. Evans was a coastwatcher, one of a small group of brave men who hid on Japanese-held islands to monitor enemy movements and arrange

rescue missions for downed airmen and shipwrecked sailors. The Navy had already radioed Evans asking for all available information about the missing PT-109.

Kennedy scratched a message for Evans on a coconut husk, to be carried back to Evans by Biuku and Eroni. It said:

NAURO ISL

NATIVE KNOWS POSIT [ION]

HE CAN PILOT

11 ALIVE

NEED SMALL BOAT

KENNEDY

On August 7, more islanders arrived in a canoe carrying food and water and a note from Evans requesting that Kennedy return with the natives. Tucked beneath palm fronds to hide them from

ABOVE LEFT The famous coconut on which Jack carved a message for potential rescuers. ABOVE RIGHT Jack with the coconut in Palm Beach in 1944, after his discharge.

Japanese aircraft, Jack and Ross were paddled to Komu Island, where the coastwatcher made tea for the men. It was the best tea they'd ever tasted.

That night, two PT boats from Rendova picked up Kennedy and Ross. Kennedy guided them to Olsana to collect the rest of the crew, who were delivered safely to the Komu Island base by morning. Kennedy spent the next week in the sick bay, utterly worn out by the ordeal. Besides the effort of towing McMahon to safety and then swimming from island to island, he'd hardly eaten or slept in a week. But he'd brought his men back.

Jack told a friend that when he got back to base he didn't know if he'd be greeted with a medal or a court martial. After all, he'd managed to lose his ship and two men with it. Not long after the episode, and in the years since, some critics have charged that no matter how heroically Jack behaved after the ramming of PT-109, the predicament was one of his own making. He should have heard the order to withdraw from Blackett Strait. Or, if he'd posted proper lookouts, the Japanese destroyer would not have surprised him. Or he should have been able to maneuver PT-109 out of the way of the *Amagari* in time to avoid the collision.

But the PT's VHF radios were notoriously unreliable, and it's unclear whether specific orders were radioed to PT-109 after the initial clash with the Tokyo Express. Further, it is true that PT-109's crew wasn't on full alert—at least two were asleep—but as Ensign Ross later confirmed, there were at least five men acting as lookouts. On a moonless night, without radar, in an era before night-vision gear, it was "as dark as if you were in a closet with the door shut." Finally, PT-109 probably could have avoided the *Amagari* if its three Packard engines had been operating on full power. In fact, the boat's engines were "muffled" to reduce speed and thus diminish the boat's wake, which was a dead giveaway to Japanese patrol planes. Jack was following established procedure for PTs not in contact with the enemy.

At any rate, the Navy went the medal route. Although by the time Jack's commander's recommendations ground through the naval bureaucracy, he'd been awarded only the relatively modest Navy and Marine Corps Medal, plus a Purple Heart.

By coincidence, there were several war correspondents at the base when the PT-109 survivors came ashore, and they lost no time in turning Jack's story into a major news event. The report made the front page of the *New York Times* under the headline "Kennedy's Son Is Hero in Pacific as Destroyer Splits His PT Boat." Some months later, writer John Hersey (who, ironically, had married an old flame of Jack's, Anne Cannon) published an account of the episode, titled "Survival," in the *New Yorker*. Not satisfied with that magazine's relatively small circulation, Joe Sr. arranged for it to be published in *Reader's Digest*, and he paid for reprints out of his own pocket.

Jack could have requested a transfer stateside, but he chose to stay in the combat zone. He felt he still had a job to do—and he wanted to give the Japanese some payback. He took command of a new boat, PT-59, went on some more missions, and saw some more action. But his back and stomach were still in bad shape. He'd contracted malaria while in the South Pacific, and an X-ray turned up what looked like a duodenal ulcer. His commander sent him home. Jack went ashore in San Francisco on January 7, 1944, after seventeen months in the South Pacific.

STATESIDE . . . AND TRAGEDY

Upon his return to the United States, Jack made his way to Palm Beach and his family via the Mayo Clinic, where doctors diagnosed the source of his stomach woes as irritable bowel syndrome—the correct diagnosis, for once. In Boston, he was told by doctors at the Lahey Clinic that he needed a back operation, which was probably a misdiagnosis. After submitting to the operation, he found himself in worse back pain than he'd felt before going under the knife. Another operation—a rectal procedure— did no good, either.

Meanwhile, from England, Joe Jr. observed his little brother's fame with a jaundiced eye. He didn't like being one-upped. In a letter to Jack, he couldn't resist some needling: "What I want to know is where the hell were you when the destroyer hove into sight?" He also reportedly burst into tears when he heard that a Boston bigwig had lauded Joe Sr. as "the father of our own hero, Lieutenant John F. Kennedy."

ABOVE Captain Frederick Conklin prepares to pin the Navy and Marine Corps Medal on Lieutenant Kennedy at Boston's Chelsea Naval Hospital on June 12, 1944. RIGHT The report of the Naval Retiring Board, citing "chronic colitis" as the main reason for Jack's discharge from the service.

JAG:1:LHCJ:mhw

RECORD OF PROCEEDINGS OF THE NAVAL RETIRING BOARD

CONVENED AT

The Navy Department, Washington, D.C., 27 December, 1944

IN THE CASE OF

Lieutenant (T) John F. Kennedy, D-V(G), U.S. Naval Reserve

NAVY DEPARTMENT
Office of the Judge Advocate General

FEB 1 5 1945

Respectfully submitted.

The findings of the Board in this case are as follows:

"The board, having deliberated on the evidence before it, decided that Lieutenant John F. Kennedy, D-V(G), U. S. Naval Reserve, is incapacitated for active service in the Naval Reserve by reason of colitis, chronic; that this incapacity for naval service is permanent, and is the result of an incident of the service, having been incurred subsequent to October 27, 1941, and suffered in line of duty from disease or injury while employed on active duty, pursuant to orders contemplating extended naval service in excess of thirty days.

"The board considers that this officer's incapacity was incurred subsequent to October 20, 1943, the effective date of commencement of service in the grade of Lieutenant, to which grade he had been appointed for temporary service in time of war or national emergency."

The record was referred to the Chiefs of the Bureau of Medicine and Surgery and Naval Personnel and was returned recommending approval of the findings of the Board in this case.

In the opinion of this office, the proceedings and findings of the Board in this case are legal.

Acting Judge Advocate General of the Navy.

NAVY DEPARTMENT
Office of the Judge Advocate General

MAR 5 1945

The record of proceedings of the Naval Retiring Board in the case of Lieutenant (T) John F. Kennedy, D-V(G), U.S. Naval Reserve, - - was transmitted to the Secretary of the Navy, and by him laid before the President for his approval or disapproval, or orders in the case, with the recommendation that the findings of the Board be approved and that Lieutenant (T) John F. Kennedy, D-V(G), U.S. Naval Reserve, be retired from active service and placed on the retired list, in conformity with the provisions of 34 U.S. Code 417, 855c-1 and 350g(a).

On   FEB 2 8 1945   , the President approved the proceedings and findings of the Naval Retiring Board and the recommendation of the Secretary of the Navy.

L. H. C. JOHNSON

For Judge Advocate General of the Navy.

U. S. GOVERNMENT PRINTING OFFICE   16—27313-1

By now Joe Jr. was a naval aviator, flying long, boring antisubmarine patrols over the Atlantic and seeing no action. By the summer of 1944, he'd flown more than the number of missions required to go home. He wasn't prepared to return home without an exploit—and a medal to match or exceed his little brother's. So he volunteered for a top-secret and extremely dangerous mission—a mission that, if he survived, would earn him the Silver Star, maybe even the Navy Cross, the highest medal that can be awarded by the Navy.

German V-1 flying bombs were now falling on London. The Navy came up with the idea of packing old B-24 bombers full of explosives and crashing them into V-1 launch sites on the Belgian coast. The pilot and copilot would bail out over the English Channel at the last minute, to be fished out by patrol craft.

On the evening of August 12, 1944, Joe Jr. took off in a B-24 crammed with 20,000 pounds of TNT. The plane hadn't even reached the English coast before it exploded. Most likely, frequency interference from coastal radar stations caused the explosives to detonate prematurely. The plane, Joe Jr., and his copilot were literally atomized.

News of their oldest son's death reached the Kennedy compound at Hyannis Port the following afternoon. After the initial shock, Rose took comfort in her religion. Joe Sr. tried to be stoic, but it was clear to observers that the loss of his first-born son, on whom he'd pinned so many hopes, shook him to the core of his being. He never really got over it, sometimes choking up, even years later, at the very

ABOVE Savoring a cigar, Jack relaxes at Palm Beach after returning home a Navy hero. RIGHT A letter from Jack's congressional secretary describes his plans to fly to England to attend Kick's funeral in May 1948. In the end, it was Joe Sr. alone who represented the family.

mention of Joe Jr.'s name. In a way, Jack never got over it, either. He wrote to Lem Billings, "I'm shadow-boxing in a match [that] the shadow is always going to win."

Just three years later, Joe Jr.'s death was followed by that of another sibling. Kick had remained behind in England during the war, where she'd fallen in love with Billy Hartington, a young—and Protestant—aristocrat and army officer. The devout Rose shunned Kick when they married. Hartington fell to a sniper's bullet in September 1944. Four years later, Kick announced she was in love again. Peter Milford was also an English aristocrat and also a Protestant—and he was married, too, though he planned to divorce his wife to marry Kick. It was Rose's worst nightmare.

The marriage never came to pass. On May 15, 1948, while en route to a skiing vacation, the plane carrying Kick and Milford crashed in France. There were no survivors.

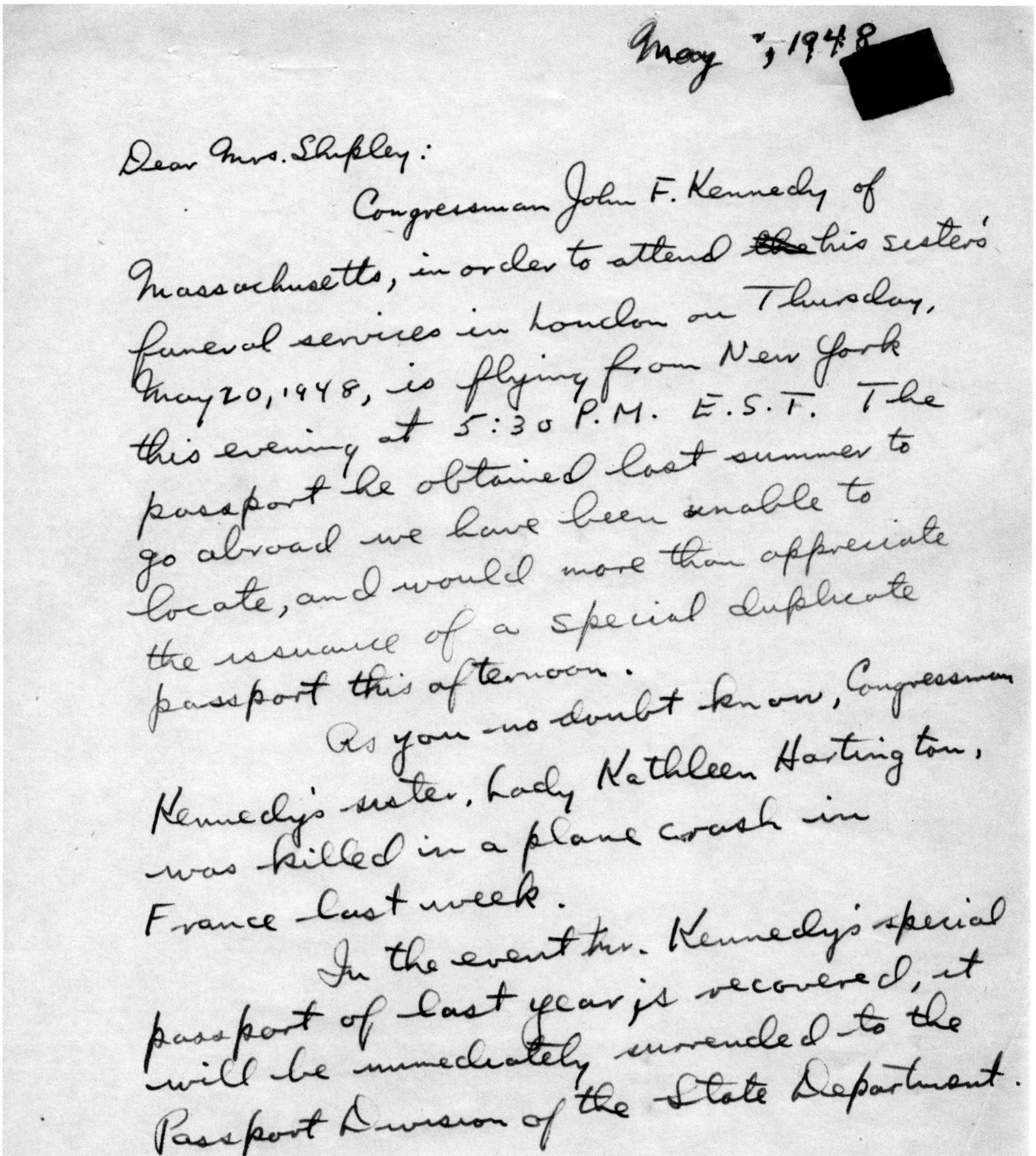

> May *, 1948
>
> Dear Mrs. Shipley:
>
> Congressman John F. Kennedy of Massachusetts, in order to attend ~~the~~ his sister's funeral services in London on Thursday, May 20, 1948, is flying from New York this evening at 5:30 P.M. E.S.T. The passport he obtained last summer to go abroad we have been unable to locate, and I would more than appreciate the issuance of a special duplicate passport this afternoon.
>
> As you no doubt know, Congressman Kennedy's sister, Lady Kathleen Hartington, was killed in a plane crash in France last week.
>
> In the event Mr. Kennedy's special passport of last year is recovered, it will be immediately surrendered to the Passport Division of the State Department.
>
> Sincerely,
> T. L. Reardon Jr
> Secretary to Cong. Kennedy

The conventional historical view is that with Joe Jr. gone, Joe Sr. turned to a reluctant Jack and told him that now it was up to him to enter politics with the goal of becoming the first Catholic president. The reality may be more complicated. Jack would later claim that his father doubted whether he had what it took to succeed in politics, and that *he*, Jack, had to persuade his father that he was up to it. Indeed, to an observer, it might well seem that Jack's basically cerebral personality wasn't up to the challenges of politics—especially the shoulder-slapping, hail-fellow-well-met world of Massachusetts politics.

Jack was not, at first, a particularly inspiring speaker or skillful debater. He also didn't like to be touched, and pressing the flesh on the campaign trail was a trial. But he worked hard to acquire the necessary skills to be a politician. Essentially, he would create a new public persona for himself—one he dubbed "the BP," for "Big Personality." It helped that he was photogenic, and as it turned out, also well suited to the new medium of television.

Just what position he would run for, and when, was still undecided. First, he would spend time at an Arizona resort, where he focused on his health and on finishing his second book, *As We Remember Joe,* a memorial to his fallen brother that was privately printed for friends and family.

JOHN FITZGERALD KENNEDY

INTERNATIONAL NEWS SERVICE

By April 1945, German troops were being beaten back by the Western Allies and Soviet troops, and the Nazis were on the verge of surrendering. The Allied countries had been united under a 1942 declaration that established the notion of the United Nations, and on April 25, 1945, brought together fifty governments in San Francisco to draft the Charter of the United Nations. Joe Sr. set up a reporting job for Jack to cover this first meeting of the United Nations for the Chicago *Herald-American* newspaper. By the time that assignment ended, the war in Europe was over (though American forces were still engaged in war with Japan) and the *Herald-American* sent Jack overseas to survey what was left of the continent. In England, he was thrilled to follow his hero Winston Churchill on his platform speeches. In Germany, he witnessed up close the devastation of six years of war and learned of the appalling behavior of Soviet troops in the country's eastern occupation zone. Jack returned to the States just in time to hear news of America's atomic bombing of Japan.

With his political education rounded out, and any idealism shaken by the realities of war, Jack was prepared to run for his first publicly appointed position. His first political battle would be for the 1946

ABOVE Jack's business card from the International News Service. RIGHT An article by Jack written in 1945 shows that he had grown capable of turning out quite pithy, energetic writing—in contrast to the somewhat stilted prose of *Why England Slept.*

Serviceman's View of Conference:

Soviet Diplomacy Gets 50-50 Break

(Lt. John F. Kennedy, recently retired PT Boat hero of the South Pacific and son of Former Ambassador Joseph P. Kennedy, is covering the San Francisco United Nations Conference from a serviceman's point of view for the N. Y. Journal-American. Before the war he authored the best seller "Why England Slept.")

By JOHN F. KENNEDY
Special to the N. Y. Journal-American

SAN FRANCISCO, May 3.—The word is out more or less officially that Molotov is about to pick up his marbles and go home. He'll leave his delegation here to carry out the important detailed work. This news comes as no surprise because as the spotlight turns toward Europe and the war's ending—not only Molotov but many of the reporters are getting ready to head east.

Diplomacy might be said to be the art of who gets what and how as applied to international affairs. As Mr. Molotov gets ready to leave, Lets look at Mr. Molotov's record and see what he got and how he went about it.

His record as far as what he got was .500. He won the fight over chairmanship and the fight for the inclusion of White Russia and the Ukraine while he lost on Poland and the Argentine.

LT. JOHN F. KENNEDY

RUSSIAN DIPLOMACY.

This last fight over Argentina has been hailed as a moral victory for him but it remains to be seen how much they pay off on moral victories.

This battle, however, is worth examining as it gives good insight into Russian diplomacy at this conference.

The maneuvering really began on the second day of the conference when a reporter asked Mr. Molotov whether he was in favor of admitting Argentina to the United Nations Conference.

He replied with what appeared sincere surprise that that was "a new question" for him and that he had no comment. Yet four days later he waged a bitter battle on the assembly floor against Argentina being admitted to the conference.

CHANGE IN ATTITUDE.

What caused thi change of attitude?

The most popularly accepted theory is that he thought that by making a fight over it he could win a compromise and bring Poland in on Argentina's coat-tails.

Now no one here held any particular brief for Argentina's conduct during the war — but the South Americans did want her in. It was their belief that any Fascist tendencies that Argentina might have could be controlled better if she was joined with them than if she went her way alone.

They also felt that since she had been admitted to the conference at Chapultepec with President Roosevelt's OK, she should also be admitted here. Some of the European countries went along realizing that Argentine food and supplies could be a big help in rehabilitating Europe.

Democratic nomination for U.S. Representative from Boston's Eleventh District. This district, while it included Harvard, was a mostly working-class Irish and Italian enclave and solidly Democratic. The Eleventh's current Representative was none other than Honey Fitz's old nemesis, James M. Curley, who was also serving as mayor. Curley decided not to run for reelection in the Eleventh (possibly thanks to some financial incentive from Joe Sr.), which left the road clearer for Jack to clinch the Democratic nomination.

However, Jack would face a motley crew of ten challengers in the Democratic primary campaign, and victory was by no means assured. He would need the help of family and friends. Jack was a war hero and the Kennedy name carried a lot of weight in the district. His opponents charged that he was a rich man's son "throwing his diaper into the ring." They opposed the fact that he was just twenty-nine and he hadn't lived in Boston for twenty years. Jack countered these jabs with an unaffected wit. At one rally, each speaker was introduced with variations on the theme of "Our next speaker came up the hard way." When Jack took the podium, he told the crowd, "I seem to be the only person here tonight who *didn't* come up the hard way," a remark that was greeted with much laughter.

The campaign was run by a mix of seasoned Irish pols, Jack's friends (including, at various times, Red Fay, Torby Macdonald, and Lem Billings), plus some new faces, including political operatives Dave Powers and Joe Kane. Kane provided the campaign's slogan, "The New Generation Offers a Leader." Joe Sr. operated behind the scenes, dispensing cash as needed and making sure every household in the district got a copy of John Hersey's *New Yorker* piece about PT-109. Rose and Eunice organized a reception for the district's women voters at the Commander Hotel, sending out engraved invitations to women who, in biographer Michael O'Brien's words, "had never received an engraved invitation to anything in their lives." The event was a huge success.

No one worked harder or longer than the candidate himself. In a back brace, pounding up and down the stairs of the district's three-decker houses was an ordeal, as was standing outside factory gates shaking hundreds of workers' hands at shift changes. Jack spoke to every civic, fraternal, and

LEFT The skinny young veteran leads a parade during his 1946 congressional campaign. Note that he carries, rather than wears his hat—Jack never liked to wear headgear. ABOVE Jack speaking at one of the many campaign events of 1946.

religious group that would hear him. On the day before the primary, he collapsed in the August sun while marching in a parade in Charlestown. He looked so bad that onlookers feared he'd had a heart attack, but it was just sunstroke and exhaustion.

Jack was fully recovered by the following night when the returns came in. He won the nomination handily. When news of his victory came, eighty-three-year-old Honey Fitz danced a jig and broke into "Sweet Adeline." Jack cruised to victory in the general election and began the first of three terms (he would run unopposed in the 1948 and 1950 Democratic primaries back in Boston) in the U.S. House of Representatives.

CONGRESSMAN KENNEDY

Jack moved into a house in Georgetown, which he shared with his sister Eunice. Their home became a kind of frat house for younger legislators, their staffers, and other best-and-brightest types. This was just a prelude to the lively intellectual and cultural scene that would characterize the Kennedy White House.

As a Congressman, Kennedy's legislative record was mixed. He sometimes called himself a liberal conservative. On domestic issues, he showed a staunch devotion to the principles of FDR's New Deal. His first speech in the House, in fact, was a denunciation of the proposed Taft-Hartley Act, which would do away with many of the gains organized labor had won during Roosevelt's administration. To his dismay and despite his objections, the measure ultimately made it into law. Befitting someone who'd run on the strength of his veteran status, Kennedy also spent a lot of time on veteran's affairs, including proposing federal aid to provide housing for the millions of returning veterans and their families.

When it came to foreign policy, however, Kennedy was a definite conservative, and he took a hard line against communist expansion. His years in the House coincided with the start of the Cold War. When the Soviet Union came to dominate Eastern Europe and acquire the atomic bomb, communism took hold in China, and a hot war erupted in Korea. Kennedy's anticommunism won him some supporters on the other side of the aisle, including Richard Nixon of California, another Navy veteran just four years Kennedy's senior.

Indeed, Kennedy believed that "foreign policy—in its impact on our daily lives—overshadows everything." This conviction certainly motivated his frequent travel abroad. Also, Jack was simply bored by the legislative routine of the House. While he won the admiration of many of his congressional colleagues for his intelligence and ability, he was never known as a very hard-working congressman. His attendance record was so poor, there was a running joke that when the House Minority Leader, John McCormack, met him in the House, McCormack greeted him by saying, "Nice of you to

RIGHT The strain of the congressional campaign showing in his gaunt face, Jack unwinds with one of the several dogs that had the run of the Hyannis Port compound, 1946.

stop by and see us, John." Visitors to his office were more likely to find him practicing his putting than poring over the fine print of a bill.

It was on his many trips that Jack's sicknesses often got the best of him. In the summer of 1947, he set out for Europe as part of a Congressional delegation sent to investigate Soviet influence on labor unions in the struggling democracies of Western Europe. First, he stopped in Ireland, where he

ABOVE Wearing a too-big pin-striped suit, Jack poses with Honey Fitz, Rose, and Mrs. Fitzgerald.

hoped to connect with his Irish heritage. He was joined by Pamela Digby Churchill, formerly Winston Churchill's daughter-in-law. Jack insisted they drive into the countryside so he could try to find some trace of his ancestral family, but there were too many Kennedys to establish any connection. Unfortunately, he never made it to continental Europe. Arriving in London, he fell so ill that he couldn't get out of bed. An eminent British medico, Sir Daniel Davis, immediately diagnosed Addison's disease.

Addison's disease is a progressive deterioration of the adrenal glands. When the adrenal glands fail, they stop secreting hormones like aldosterone and cortisol that the body needs to maintain glucose levels, blood pressure, and other vital functions. Until the 1930s, a diagnosis of Addison's was a de facto death sentence; sufferers rarely lasted more than a year. In that decade, an artificial form of adrenal hormone, DOCA, was developed, and it was found to extend life expectancy. Dr. Davis told Pamela Digby that Jack probably wouldn't last a year, even with the new DOCA treatment.

It was Jack's worst health crisis to date—and one that his staff took special cautions to hide from the public and the media. He was carried aboard the liner *Queen Mary* on a stretcher for an immediate return to the States. The story given to the press was that Representative Kennedy was suffering a recurrence of the malaria he'd picked up in the Pacific. His condition got so bad that at one point, a priest was brought in to administer the last rites.

But Jack made it back to the United States, where a private plane flew him to Boston for his first round of DOCA therapy. The procedure involved doctors making an incision into his thigh and inserting a pellet of the artificial adrenal hormone. Until the introduction of an oral form of hydrocortisone several years later, Jack would have to endure this procedure every couple of months. The doctors told him that with luck, he could expect to live to see age forty or forty-five.

When his health allowed, Jack traveled extensively during the remainder of his stint in the House—Israel and India, Pakistan and Malaya, Tokyo and Thailand, Yugoslavia and Indochina. On a worldwide trip in 1951, his Addison's flared up seriously (perhaps because of his habit of leaving behind or forgetting to take his medications). He arrived in a Navy hospital on Okinawa in a coma. Once again, a priest administered the last rites. And once again, Jack recovered with remarkable speed and resumed the journey.

Even as he broadened his horizons, taking in the world and solidifying his foreign-policy convictions, Kennedy needed a challenge. He needed statewide office, something beyond the House of Representatives, like governor or senator. He preferred senator, goaded a bit by the fact that two of his contemporaries were already in the upper house: his friend and fellow Democrat George Smathers of Florida and Richard Nixon. The next senate race in Massachusetts was in 1952. Kennedy faced a potential and formidable opponent in the incumbent governor, Paul Devers, who was contemplating a run for the senate. In April 1952, however, Devers announced he'd seek another term as governor, which left the road open for Kennedy to become the Democratic candidate.

But it would be a tough road. Kennedy had to make his case not just to his current constituents, the voters of Boston's Eleventh District, but also to the whole state. Massachusetts was a diverse state

Enclosures

LETTER A heartfelt love note from "Binga" to Jack, scandalously printed on *Times Herald* letterhead. PRESS RELEASE Congressman Kennedy's report on his trip to the Middle and Far East reveals the state of America's foreign affairs and Kennedy's thoughts on Communism.

ABOVE A snapshot taken during Jack's 1952 Senate campaign. RIGHT A 1951 memo listing the countries Jack intended to visit.

ENNEDY, JOHN FITZGERALD — REP. — MASS.

Will apply in Boston

Leaving Middle of September

Western Europe
~~Spain~~ 2
~~Germany~~

✓ India — Study VISA .
Thailand — no visa required
Malaya (British) ✓
Vietnam (Indo-China) (France) ✓ Saigon ?
✓ Pakistan ✓ MC
~~Afghanistan~~ 4
✓ Indonesia OK
✓ Australia OK
~~Philippines~~ 3
Iran
Siam — Burma OK

28 VISA forms for Afghan, Spain & Philippines to miss Davis.

4 Miss Davis does not know of M.C. plans. Will advise no later
6 " " State M.C. has not yet applied for ppt in Bo
11/51 file to m Siegel's section.   10/1 Issued germ'y V

3/51 Miss Davis says — get above visas.
3 Ppt to Koch
1 Miss Davis ~~to obt~~ doesn't know when M C will leave.

1 Ppt — via Rem-Stop to M.C. For   Miss Mary Davis
     signature & info re countries to be
                                visited

                                Room 322
                                House Office Bldg.

27 Kirk — m Israel, Iran, Singapore, Indo-china, India
7 Japan form to Mrs White

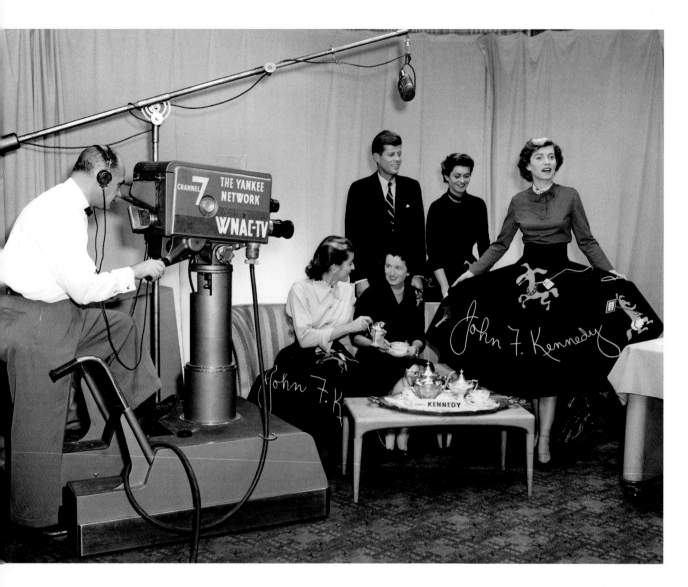

including French-Canadian mill workers, Portuguese fishermen, African Americans and Jews in inner-city Boston, and the old-line Protestant Yankees in the rural counties. And his opponent was formidable. Republican Henry Cabot Lodge Jr. was descended from one of the state's oldest families, was a Boston Brahmin to his fingertips, and was also popular and vastly more experienced than Kennedy.

Kennedy and his family's political machine campaigned tirelessly through 1952. Rose and Eunice hosted no fewer than thirty-five tea receptions for women voters. Joe Sr. was quick to see the possibilities of television, and not only did Jack appear on TV, Rose proved to be the small-screen star of this campaign, hosting two morning *Coffee with the Kennedys* programs that were big hits. Unfortunately, during Jack's first broadcast, a TelePrompTer malfunction left him floundering for words. But this small glitch didn't jeopardize his campaign. Ultimately, Kennedy took the state by about 70,000 votes.

ABOVE The Kennedy women model the latest in 1950s fashion—the John F. Kennedy poodle skirt—on television, 1952. RIGHT Kennedy's Oath of Office as a United States Senator.

In the Senate of the United States

January 3, 1953

I, John F. Kennedy, do solemnly swear (or affirm) that I will support and defend the Constitution of the United States against all enemies, foreign and domestic; that I will bear true faith and allegiance to the same; that I take this obligation freely, without any mental reservation or purpose of evasion; and that I will well and faithfully discharge the duties of the office on which I am about to enter: So help me God.

John F. Kennedy

Subscribed and sworn to before me this 3rd day of January, A. D. 1953

Alben W. Barkley
President of the Senate.

State Massachusetts

FAMILY MAN *and* MODERN CAMPAIGNER

3.

JACK'S BACHELOR STATUS, combined with his youth and good looks, formed part of his appeal. He was constantly being named one of Washington's (or Congress's) most eligible bachelors in newspapers and magazines. As he approached his mid-thirties, he was drawing nearer to the age when a politician with national ambitions would be expected to start a family. The congressman needed a wife.

Any bride of Jack's would have to meet his father's criteria. She would have to be Catholic, of course. Ideally, she would come from a "good family"—Joe Sr. remained insecure about his own family's place in the social hierarchy. In 1950, Arthur Krock told Joe Sr. he knew a young woman who fit the bill. One night in 1951, Jack attended a dinner party at the home of journalist Charles Bartlett and his wife, Mary. Among the other guests was a slender, black-haired, husky-voiced beauty named Jackie Bouvier. At the behest of Joe Kennedy and Arthur Krock, the Bartletts were playing matchmaker.

Jacqueline Lee Bouvier was born in the exclusive Long Island enclave of Southampton in 1929 to John Bouvier III, known as "Black Jack," and Janet Lee Bouvier. The family liked to claim descent from French nobility and colonial Virginia aristocracy, but in fact, the background on both sides was modest. Black Jack made a fortune as a stockbroker in the 1920s, only to lose much of it after the

LEFT Senator and Mrs. John F. Kennedy cutting the cake following their wedding on September 12, 1953.

ABOVE Senator Kennedy's bachelor status was a keen source of interest in the newspapers. Many single women tried to change that status; Evelyn Lincoln, his secretary, later said that "The women chased him . . . half my telephone calls were [from] women."

Crash of 1929. As his bank balance fell, his already considerable drinking and womanizing increased. In 1940, Black Jack and Janet divorced, and shortly afterward, Janet remarried to a wealthy banker, Hugh D. Auchincloss, known as "Hughdie."

The Auchinclosses divided their time between estates in Virginia and Rhode Island, and Jackie and her younger sister Lee grew up in the privileged world of the east coast elite. Jackie excelled at horseback riding and developed an interest in literature and art. Her education was straight out of the social register: Chapin School in New York City, Miss Porter's School in Connecticut, a couple of years at Vassar College, her junior year abroad at the Sorbonne in Paris, rounded out by George Washington University, from which she graduated with a degree in French Literature in 1951. In an odd echo of the Inga Arvad episode, Arthur Krock arranged an "Inquiring Camera Girl" job for Jackie at the Washington *Times-Herald* newspaper.

ABOVE Jackie and her mother on horseback sometime in the 1930s. Jackie was a very accomplished equestrienne, winning several national competitions before she was in her teens. RIGHT Jackie, the "Inquiring Camera Girl," at work (for which she was paid $42.50 per week), circa 1952.

Jack and Jackie's initial meeting didn't bode particularly well. For one thing, Jackie was already engaged—though her mother forced her to break off that relationship because the young man in question was insufficiently rich. But a chord had been struck. About a year later, Jack and Jackie found themselves at another dinner party at the Bartletts. As Jack remembered it, "I leaned across the asparagus and asked her for a date."

A slow and sporadic courtship followed. Jackie was spending a lot of time in Europe, and Jack was busy with his Senate campaign—and with other women. Their dates were mostly evenings spent playing board games or discussing books; a passion for reading was one of the few things the two had in common. In the summer of 1952, Jackie began appearing at Jack's campaign rallies, and in January 1953, she attended President Dwight Eisenhower's inaugural ball on Jack's arm.

Over the course of their courtship, Jackie got to know the Kennedys' private world, and she didn't like everything she saw. Jackie loathed the intense atmosphere at Hyannis Port, where everything— from dinner-table conversation to touch football—turned into a bruising competition. "They never relax," she later said, "not even when they're relaxing." Her relationship with Rose was civil but chilly;

the two never warmed to one another. Jack's sisters interpreted Jackie's reserved nature as snobbishness and mocked her behind her back. For her part, Jackie dismissed Jack's female siblings as "the rah-rah girls."

But Jackie got on like a house on fire with Joe Sr., and ultimately, that was what mattered. In Lem Billings's words, "Joe not only approved the marriage—he ordained it." Jackie's mother was all for the match, too. By now Hughdie Auchincloss's fortune wasn't what it once was. Janet was determined that her daughters would never want for money, and marrying a Kennedy seemed a sure way to guarantee Jackie would be well cared for.

Despite the machinations that brought them together, Jack and Jackie's marriage was in no sense a "marriage of convenience." There was a deep connection between the two. As Jack told Red Fay, "I've known a lot of attractive women in my lifetime before I got married, but of all of them there was

ABOVE Jack and Jackie announced their engagement in June 1953. This is their "official" engagement photo. RIGHT The newly engaged couple at Hyannis Port. The cerebral Jackie was never very comfortable around Jack's boisterous family.

only one I could have married—and I married her." Jackie was a very intelligent woman, and intelligence was a quality that Jack rated highly. The two also had similar personalities. Jackie once described herself and her husband as a "pair of icebergs." Both could be outwardly charming, but they valued their privacy and were somewhat self-contained emotionally.

Jack had discussed marriage with Jackie for some time, but he didn't formally propose until May 1953—by telegram, as Jackie was in England. She wired back her acceptance, and the date was set for September 12. In July, Jack, accompanied by his friend and former Harvard roommate Torbert "Torby" Macdonald, headed to the south of France for a final bachelor fling, much to Jackie's annoyance.

The wedding, expertly stage-managed by Joe Sr. for maximum publicity, was as much a public spectacle as a private celebration. Five hundred people attended the ceremony at St. Mary's Roman Catholic Church in Greenwich, Connecticut, which was led by Archbishop Richard Cushing, a powerful prelate sometimes called "the Kennedy family's parish priest." A lavish reception was held for several hundred more at Hammersmith Farm, one of the Auchincloss estates, in Newport, Rhode Island.

The wedding appeared to go off without a hitch, even though Jack arrived at the church with scratches on his face from one of the Kennedys' trademark touch football games the night before. He was also in agony from back pain during the long ceremony, with its constant kneeling and rising. Jackie, for her part, was hurt to discover that her father, with whom she was very close, would not be

walking her down the aisle. That honor went to Hughdie Auchincloss instead. The official explanation was that Black Jack Bouvier was "ill." In fact, he was drunk. He may even have been plied with drink in a deliberate effort to exclude him from the ceremony.

After a honeymoon in Mexico, Jack and Jackie set up house in Washington. The early years of their marriage were a difficult time for the new Mrs. John F. Kennedy. While she'd known about Jack's womanizing at least in a general way before his proposal, dealing with his behavior as his wife was a trial. And while Jackie would soon prove to be one of Jack's greatest political assets, she entered into the marriage without really grasping what it would mean to be the spouse of a public figure. One day not long after the wedding, she overheard Joe, Jack, and his brother Robert brainstorming about how Jackie could best help Jack in his quest for the White House. She realized with horror that at one level, she was seen as nothing more than an asset in her new husband's political portfolio. As she put it to a friend, "They spoke of me as if I wasn't a person."

LEFT The bride wore an ivory silk taffeta gown designed by Ann Lowe, an African-American dressmaker, and a lace veil handed down from her grandmother. ABOVE The wedding party poses at Newport.

MCCARTHY AND MISERY

In 1953, Senator Kennedy and his fellow members of the upper chamber were moving toward a showdown. Republican senator Joseph McCarthy, a former chicken farmer who was elected to the Senate from Wisconsin in 1946, was becoming an increasingly prominent figure in the anti-communist movement.

Communism's success abroad in the late 1940s and early 1950s—China had established itself as a communist nation and the Soviet Union had grown to encompass much of Eastern Europe—created a climate of fear at home. Conservatives in both parties, along with the right-wing press, charged that Soviet agents were subverting the federal government, the nation's universities, and Hollywood from within. As early as 1947, the Truman administration instituted loyalty oaths for government employees. Around the same time, Richard Nixon, Jack's fellow freshman in the congressional class of 1946, won nationwide fame as a member of HUAC (the House Committee on Un-American Activities), in which capacity he oversaw the conviction, on perjury charges, of a respected State Department official named Alger Hiss, who was suspected of being a Soviet agent.

Politicians and journalists brave enough to speak up denounced the activities of HUAC and other organizations as witch hunts. But the paranoia that had taken hold of the country had many Americans believing that people who stood up for the constitutional rights of accused communists might be "reds" too.

In 1950, McCarthy produced a paper that he claimed listed hundreds of communists in the State Department. While Soviet agents had actually infiltrated the government, McCarthy and his co-conspirators had no way of knowing this. This fact would only be confirmed four decades later after the end of the Cold War. McCarthy's famous list was a complete fiction, but it was a shrewd way for him to exploit a culture of fear in order to advance his own career.

By the time Kennedy was elected to the Senate, McCarthy had started to overreach himself. His wild charges grew to include revered figures like former World War II Army Chief of Staff and Secretary of State George Marshall. Televised hearings over McCarthy's accusations of communist influence in the Army revealed him to be an ignorant bully. Although he retained much of his popularity with the public, by 1953, McCarthy was increasingly regarded by his fellow members of the Senate as a colossal embarrassment. A movement was afoot to introduce a measure of censure against McCarthy for bringing the Senate, according to their censure resolution, "into dishonor and disrepute."

In 1953, a group of Massachusetts citizens sent Kennedy a letter asking him to state his position on the growing anti-McCarthy movement in the Senate. He sent back an uncharacteristically wishy-washy reply: "I assure you that I am giving attention to this situation, and I am hopeful that the outcome will be the most desirable for the good of the country." Kennedy's friends and political associates

TOP LEFT The newlyweds enjoyed a two-week honeymoon in Acapulco, Mexico. BOTTOM LEFT The couple tools around the streets of Acapulco. They returned to Washington by way of Los Angeles and San Francisco.

had no doubt where he stood on McCarthy—he loathed both the man and his methods—but McCarthy was a hero to many of Kennedy's constituents in Massachusetts, particularly Irish Catholics, who were willing to overlook the fact that he was a Republican in favor of his Celtic surname and Catholic faith.

Indeed, Joe Sr. was a huge admirer of McCarthy. He contributed to McCarthy's campaign coffers, invited him to the Kennedy home at Palm Beach, and even attended McCarthy's wedding, along with Bobby Kennedy. Bobby was even more closely associated with McCarthy and in 1952 worked as assistant counsel on McCarthy's Senate Permanent Committee on Sub-Investigations. Bobby remained on the job only seven months before resigning after a dispute with fellow counsels Roy Cohn and G. David Schine, but he and McCarthy remained close friends.

Jack knew he risked the wrath of his father and brother, as well as a substantial number of his constituents, if he said "yea" when the censure resolution came to a vote, and the decision left him deeply conflicted. As a representative, he'd investigated communist influence on labor unions, but he was far more focused on the real threat of communism overseas than the perceived threat of communism at home. When it came to civil rights, in fact, he had a strong libertarian streak. In 1949, he opposed legislation making it easier for the federal government to obtain authorization for wiretapping, and a year later, he sternly warned the graduating class of the University of Notre Dame that the growing power of the federal government posed a danger to America's traditional liberties.

While the censure resolution loomed, Jack's health again nosedived. By now, his back had deteriorated to the point where he would likely be in a wheelchair permanently in a few years. He elected for surgery to shore up his decaying vertebrae with a metal plate. It was a risky procedure for anyone. For someone with Addison's disease, which left his body very susceptible to infection despite his cortisone therapy, it meant a fifty-fifty chance of survival at best. A tearful Joe Sr. begged him not to go through with it, reminding his son that Franklin Roosevelt had reached the White House in a wheelchair.

But Jack went ahead. Even as he was prepped for surgery on October 21, 1954, McCarthy was on his mind. He told Chuck Spalding, "You know, when I go downstairs, I know exactly what's going to happen. Those reporters are going to lean over my stretcher . . . And then every one of those guys is going to say, 'Now, Senator, what about McCarthy?' And I'm going to pull the sheet over my head and yell 'Ow!'"

After the operation, it seemed likely that the patient would require a shroud, not a sheet. A staph infection set in and Kennedy slipped into a coma. A priest was summoned. Jackie prayed aloud at his bedside. And against the odds, as he had twice before, he came back from the brink of death. Jack's survival was so unusual that the case was written up in a medical journal—though the patient's name was not identified. The public still didn't know the truth about his condition. Press releases said Jack was undergoing routine surgery for a PT-109-related injury.

LEFT The newlywed senator in Washington, where he and Jackie rented a house on Dent Avenue in Georgetown.

The censure resolution against McCarthy came to a vote on December 2, 1954, while Jack was still in the hospital. It passed by a margin of 67 to 22. The Democratic vote against McCarthy was unanimous. The vote of only one senator—John F. Kennedy (D-Mass.)—went unrecorded.

Obviously, Kennedy had the excuse of being in slow recovery from a major operation to explain his unrecorded vote. But while the operation had ravaged his body, his mind was perfectly clear, and under senatorial procedure, he could have voted in absentia. One of his aides, Ted Sorensen, would later say, "I think that [Kennedy] deliberately did not contact me" about what to do, though at the time, Sorensen said that the fault was his, that he could have sent Kennedy's vote in for the record.

A couple of years later, a speech written by Kennedy but never delivered appeared in newspapers and revealed that he would have voted for censure. In the paper, he clarified that his position was not

to condemn "the motives or the sincerity of the junior senator from Wisconsin." The speech justified support for censure solely on the narrow and legalistic grounds that Kennedy opposed "certain practices in which he [McCarthy] acquiesced." It was thin gruel. In the words of Michael O'Brien, "The ghost of Joe McCarthy continued to plague [Jack's] career." McCarthy would indeed be a ghost before long. He died of complications of alcoholism in 1957.

PROFILES IN COURAGE

Jack's initial back surgery, which involved screwing a metal plate into his spine, left an eight-inch-long suppurating sore on his back. In the months that followed, Jackie proved that she had some tough fiber behind her refined and delicate exterior by pitching in with the nurses to change his dressings and otherwise tend to her husband's needs.

By February 1955, it was clear the plate itself was infected, and Jack was flown back to New York from Palm Beach for another operation, in which the plate was removed and a bone graft added. By March, he was able to walk without crutches. In May, he returned to his Washington office to the glare of flashbulbs—and a fruit basket from Richard Nixon on his desk.

Jack had been away from the Senate for almost eight months. Given the long absence, there was no way to deny that he had undergone a serious ordeal, even if the Kennedy camp was vague on specifics. Over the next two years, Jack would be hospitalized on nine occasions—sometimes for a week or more at a time—for ailments including prostatitis, colitis, and more back problems. Each time, the press was given only vague details.

Besides the usual cortisone and antibiotics, Jack was now on a cocktail of medications ranging from testosterone to help him gain and keep on weight, antispasmodics for his stomach complaints, and barbiturates to help him sleep. He also started receiving injections of procaine to ease his back pain and help his mobility. This regimen was prescribed by Dr. Janet Travell, a New York neurologist who would become Jack's personal physician.

Despite his chronic conditions, Jack still projected an image of youth and vitality as he approached age forty—at least to those who didn't see him wince from pain when he got out of a chair. Ironically, his ailments and medications had something to do with this image. Addison's disease causes the skin to glow, making sufferers seem tanned, while the cortisone treatment filled out his previously gaunt face. In addition, Jack was also now dyeing his graying hair brown.

While Jack recovered from his surgeries, he turned his attention to a book project. He'd never lost his authorial ambitions. The book he conceived would tell the stories of U.S. representatives and senators who had taken unpopular stands, ignoring political considerations and instead following their personal convictions. After some dithering, Harper & Row gave Jack a contract. The book went

LEFT Senator Joseph McCarthy (rear center) and fellow senators listen to committee counsel Robert Kennedy at a hearing of the Senate Labor Committee. McCarthy had close ties to the Kennedy family—a source of trouble and embarrassment for Jack.

through several working titles—*These Brave Men, These Great Men, The Patriots*. Jack's editor finally decided it would be called *Profiles in Courage*.

While Jack literally got back on his feet at Palm Beach, his twenty-seven-year-old aide Ted Sorensen gathered research material with the help of Jules Davids, a professor at Georgetown University. Sorensen periodically flew down to Florida to work on the manuscript with his boss. Like practically everything Jack did, the writing of *Profiles* was a hurried affair. In Sorensen's slightly tongue-in-cheek words, "I doubt whether [Edward] Gibbon could have produced *The Decline and Fall of the Roman Empire* in a proportionately brief time."

Published in January 1956, *Profiles* was an immediate commercial and critical success. The review in the *Christian Science Monitor* was typical: "That a United States Senator . . . should have produced this study is as remarkable as it is helpful." The book made the *New York Times* bestseller list and sold more than 100,000 copies in eighteen months in the United States alone. *Profiles* also won Jack the Pulitzer Prize for Biography.

As with *Why England Slept*, there were whispers that *Profiles in Courage* owed its bestseller status to Joe Kennedy's buying thousands of copies and directing them to influential booksellers. Soon, a much more serious accusation surfaced: that Jack hadn't written the book at all.

In late 1957, columnist Drew Pearson stated on TV, "Jack Kennedy is . . . the only man in history that I know who won a Pulitzer Prize on a book which was ghostwritten for him." It was widely understood that the ghostwriter Pearson referred to was Ted Sorensen. A furious Jack demanded, and got, a retraction. But the question lingered: Just how much of *Profiles* was Kennedy's and how much was Sorensen's?

Profiles was in no real sense ghostwritten. The overall concept and direction were definitely Kennedy's, and there is documentary evidence—in the form of notes and dictation tapes—of his role in the actual writing. But later analyses of the book demonstrated that Sorensen was responsible for the bulk of the text. For decades, Sorensen referred to *Profiles* as "our . . . work" and described it as a "collaboration." In his 2008 memoir, *Counselor,* he finally acknowledged that the extent of his contribution was really quite considerable.

Enclosures

LETTER Representative Adam Clayton Powell Jr. of New York—one of only two African Americans in Congress at the time—sent Jack this congratulatory note upon receiving word of Jack's engagement. **NOTES** Some of Jack's handwritten notes for *Profiles in Courage*. "I never heard Jack Kennedy boast about any accomplishments or anything he had done," said his old friend from Choate, Ralph Horton, "but I could see that he was very proud . . . [of the] Pulitzer Prize award."

RIGHT A letter from Grayson Kirk, president of Columbia University, informs Jack that *Profiles in Courage* has won the Pulitzer Prize for biography.

Columbia University
in the City of New York
NEW YORK 27, N. Y.

OFFICE OF THE PRESIDENT

May 7, 1957

Senator John F. Kennedy
Senate Office Building
Washington, D. C.

Dear Senator Kennedy:

I am very happy to send you the certificate of the Pulitzer Prize in Letters for your book, "Profiles in Courage." The prize was awarded to you by action of the Trustees of Columbia University last May 6.

It is for your distinguished American biography "teaching patriotic and unselfish services to the people, illustrated by an eminent example."

Please accept my congratulations.

Sincerely yours,

Grayson Kirk

Grayson Kirk
President, Columbia University

GK/sl

Enclosure

VICE-PRESIDENTIAL BID

By the time *Profiles in Courage* hit the bookshelves, Kennedy was preparing for the next step in his political career. If he was to one day make it to the White House, the next rung on the ladder was the vice-presidency. A stint in the number-two spot would give him the national exposure and experience he needed for his own presidential bid. Nineteen fifty-six was a presidential election year, and Kennedy felt the Democrats had a good shot at regaining the presidency. The incumbent, Republican Dwight Eisenhower, had suffered a heart attack in September 1955, raising questions about his fitness for a second term. It is perhaps ironic that Kennedy felt so optimistic, given the precarious state of his own health.

ABOVE Americans for Democratic Action—a group of liberal but anticommunist Democrats whose members included Eleanor Roosevelt—supported Adlai Stevenson's nomination in 1956, a fact lampooned in this political cartoon. RIGHT Another political cartoon from the 1956 campaign depicts Jack and the Massachusetts delegation swooping down on the Democratic National Convention in Chicago.

Despite public doubts, Eisenhower quickly bounced back from his heart attack and announced that he'd seek reelection. The avuncular "Ike" was so popular that most pollsters and pundits felt that he was likely to win a second term, and he would bring his vice president, Richard Nixon, along with him. Joe Kennedy agreed with the pundits. Yet, Joe Sr. wasn't entirely unopposed to his son going for the VP nod—provided that Jack was the running-mate of the right Democratic candidate. That is, one who would likely lose, but who wouldn't get buried in an Eisenhower landslide. Kennedy needed to preserve his chances for a run at the top spot in 1960.

For the presidential nomination, Joe Kennedy favored the hard-charging Senate Majority Leader Lyndon Johnson of Texas. However, going into the Democratic National Convention, the leading contender was Adlai Stevenson, the bespectacled, balding former governor of Illinois who'd already challenged Eisenhower unsuccessfully in 1952. Stevenson was witty, articulate, and intelligent. To

many voters, these qualities marked him as an ineffectual intellectual. Joe was convinced that Stevenson would lose by a wide margin, and that if Jack were his running mate, Jack's Catholicism would be blamed for the defeat. But just as he'd gone against his father's wishes to undergo his back operation, Jack continued to actively seek the nomination.

There were several other strong contenders for the Democratic VP spot, and ultimately Stevenson sought to solve his running-mate conundrum by throwing the choice to the delegates at the convention. There were several rounds of balloting. Kennedy was in the lead at one point. In the end, the vice-presidential nomination went to Senator Estes Kefauver of Tennessee. Kennedy was sanguine, telling his father "We did our best. I've had some fun, and I didn't make a fool of myself."

In November, Eisenhower and Nixon cruised easily into a second term, defeating Stevenson and Kefauver by more than 15 percent in the popular vote. It seemed Joe was justified in his belief that if Jack had been on the ticket, his record would be forever tarnished by a major defeat in a national contest.

Still, Kennedy's run yielded some important dividends. He appeared before forty million TV viewers, and he did well, especially in his warm, off-the-cuff concession speech when he failed to clinch the VP nomination. He also won plaudits from convention delegates and viewers at home for his narration of *The Pursuit of Happiness,* a short movie about the history of the Democratic Party screened at the convention.

The Pursuit of Happiness was a slick Hollywood production, and Jack—always fascinated by Hollywood—now had a family connection to show business. In 1954, his sister Patricia married

ABOVE Jack chats with his sister Pat and brother-in-law Peter Lawford, a rising movie star, at a 1959 Los Angeles Press Club dinner. The senator's ties to Hollywood boosted his national profile. RIGHT Richard Cardinal Cushing, Archbishop of the Diocese of New York, baptizes Caroline Kennedy in Manhattan's St. Patrick's Cathedral, December 13, 1957.

British-born actor Peter Lawford. Lawford was a key member of the hard-partying "Rat Pack," which included Sammy Davis Jr., Dean Martin, Joey Bishop, and "the Chairman of the Board," Frank Sinatra. It was Lawford who approached Jack about narrating the film—maybe as a *quid pro quo* for Joe Sr.'s rumored financial contribution to the production. Over the next few years, Jack's association with this crew, combined with his youth, would give him an aura of hipness no other senator could match.

Shortly after the convention, Jack departed for a yacht cruise around the Mediterranean in the company of Torby Macdonald, his brother Teddy, and a bevy of European beauties. This escapade went on despite the fact that Jackie was eight months' pregnant. On August 23, 1956, Jackie gave birth to a stillborn daughter who would have been named Arabella had she lived. Having already suffered a miscarriage in 1955, Jackie was profoundly distraught—so distraught that Bobby, who feared that Jack's presence might only worsen matters, wired Jack that Jackie was merely "ill." Even when he learned the truth, Jack seemed in no hurry to return home. It took a stern phone call from Jack's friend and fellow senator George Smathers to get him back to the States and to Jackie's bedside.

The episode precipitated a crisis in the couple's relationship. For a time they separated, and each may have contemplated divorce. But a divorce would have doomed Jack's presidential hopes completely. Slowly, the couple rebuilt their marriage. Jackie did much of the work. She began to develop an interest in politics. She joked to a friend, "I'm learning it by osmosis." She attended her husband's committee hearings and even learned golf in an effort to connect with her husband and his political cronies.

Exasperated by the persistence of Jack's carefree bachelor attitude toward his appearance and the running of his household, Jackie put her foot down, insisting that her husband wear well-tailored two-button suits. She brought art, antiques, and sophisticated hospitality into their home on N Street in Georgetown. In her words, "I brought a certain amount of order to Jack's life. We had good food in our house—not merely the bare staples that he used to have. He no longer went out in the morning with one brown and one black shoe on. His clothes got pressed, and he got to the airport without a mad rush because I packed for him." Jack and Jackie were brought together further by the birth of their first child, a daughter named Caroline Bouvier Kennedy, in November 1957.

THE NEW FRONTIER

Throughout all of the personal and political tumult of the mid-1950s, Kennedy never took his eyes off the prize—the White House in 1960. His ambitions were well known, but many wondered why he was in such a hurry. Prominent journalist James Reston wrote in the *New York Times* in 1957, "I would tell him to slow down . . . his age is against him now; in another few years it won't be. He has time."

But Kennedy didn't think he had time. Only he, and his family and closest associates, knew the full extent of his health problems. He felt pursued by his own mortality. For Jack, the only time was now.

In the meantime, though, he had his duties as a senator. He discharged these duties with a good deal more focus and energy than he had as a representative. One of his major accomplishments was to break a twenty-year congressional deadlock over funding for the St. Lawrence Seaway, a joint U.S.–Canadian canal project that linked the Great Lakes with the St. Lawrence River. Many of his constituents opposed the Seaway, contending it would divert shipping from the Port of Boston, but Kennedy felt—correctly, as it turned out—that it would reap great economic benefits for New England as a whole and Massachusetts in particular.

Kennedy also served on the ponderously named Senate Committee to Investigate Improper Activities in the Labor Management Field, universally shortened to the Senate Rackets Committee. The committee also included Bobby Kennedy, who gained nationwide prominence for his relentless pursuit of union leaders accused of involvement with organized crime, including powerful leaders of the Teamsters Union like Dave Beck and Jimmy Hoffa.

Despite his interest in and experience with international relations, it wasn't until January 1957 that Kennedy finally got an appointment to the Senate Foreign Relations Committee. It was widely

LEFT Jack and Bobby listen to testimony during the McClellan Committee hearings of 1957. The hearings revealed the existence of a nationwide organized crime network and related corruption in labor unions.
ABOVE Another scene from the McClellan Committee hearings, popularly known as the "Racket Hearings."

thought that his earlier attempts to get on the committee were countered by Lyndon Johnson. Jack's friends joked that Johnson's initials, LBJ, stood for "let's block Jack." On defense, Jack remained relatively hawkish. He joined the Cold War chorus in claiming—despite evidence to the contrary—that there was a "missile gap" between the United States and the Soviet Union.

Kennedy's involvement in these committees made him a popular senator, and when he was up for reelection in 1958, he won a second Senate term by a margin of almost 875,000 votes—the biggest such margin in the history of Massachusetts. All the while, Jack made as many speeches, wrote as many articles, and gave as many interviews as he could, while his staff conducted surveys and wrote policy papers in an all-out effort to prep for the election of 1960.

But as 1959 gave way to 1960, many of Kennedy's friends and associates questioned his urge to run. Things seemed pretty good in the United States. Despite considerable Cold War tension, the nation had stayed out of hot war since Korea ended in 1953. The economy was doing nicely. Americans

ABOVE Jack, by now a seasoned campaigner, takes to the stump in his quest for a second Senate term.

RIGHT Brothers Jack and Bobby work the phones during Jack's 1958 senatorial reelection campaign.

were enjoying a level of prosperity never seen before. Voters didn't have much motivation for putting a Democrat in the White House. Especially one who would have to overcome concerns about his age, his religion, and the fact that he was the son of a controversial figure like Joseph Kennedy Sr. Besides all this, Kennedy's opponent would almost certainly be his sort-of friend, Richard Nixon, who had eight years' experience as vice president.

None of this swayed Kennedy from entering the race. When journalist Ben Bradlee asked him, "Do you think you can really do it?" he replied, "Yes—if I don't make a single mistake." A few days later, on January 2, 1960, Kennedy formally announced his candidacy at a press conference in the Senate Caucus Room.

The battle of the primaries began. Kennedy's chief opponents for the Democratic nod were senators Hubert Humphrey of Wisconsin and Wayne Morse of Oregon. Besides them, many of the party's liberal wing still held a torch for Adlai Stevenson, even though he wasn't officially a candidate, and others supported Lyndon Johnson.

Kennedy clinched two states in the early primaries that would be key in defeating his opponents. Wisconsin was Humphrey's home turf; Kennedy's victory there effectively ended Humphrey's candidacy and led Kennedy to joke to the press that he'd received a telegram from Joe Sr. that said, "Dear Jack: Don't buy a single vote more than is necessary. I'll help you win this election, but I'll be damned if I'm going to pay for a landslide." West Virginia, a staunchly Protestant state, forced Kennedy to confront the religion issue. His success there proved that as a Catholic, he had the power to sway Protestant voters. In one stump speech, he told the crowd, "When my brother Joe was killed in a wartime bombing mission, nobody asked if he was a Catholic."

In 1960, there were many Protestants—including influential clergymen like Norman Vincent Peale—who believed that, by definition, a Roman Catholic president's first loyalty would be to the Pope, not the Constitution of the United States. What's more, many members of Kennedy's own party—Catholics and non-Catholics alike—retained bitter memories of New York governor Al Smith's stinging defeat by Protestant Republican Herbert Hoover in the 1928 presidential election.

Kennedy defused the religion issue with great rhetorical skill and sensitivity. The event that ultimately rendered his religion irrelevant was the brilliant speech Kennedy made to an association of Protestant clergy in Houston on September 12, 1960:

> *I believe in an America where the separation of church and state is absolute; where no Catholic prelate would tell the President—should he be Catholic—how to act, and no Protestant minister would tell his parishioners for whom to vote; where no church or church school is granted any public funds or political preference, and where no man is denied public office merely because his religion differs from the President who might appoint him, or the people who might elect him.*

LEFT John Vachon took this photo of Jack in his rocking chair for *Look* magazine in August 1959. Jack eventually had fourteen such chairs, all made by the P & P Furniture Co. of North Carolina, in his various homes and offices.

SEE AND HEAR

SENATOR AND MRS.

John F. Kennedy

AT
GLENWOOD PARK

Tuesday, April 26, 1960

7:30 P. M.

MUSIC BY

Gordon Jennings and his Band

... Refreshments Will Be Served ...

SPONSORED BY
WEST VIRGINIANS FOR KENNEDY
COMMITTEE

After Wisconsin and West Virginia, Kennedy's victories in the next couple of primaries essentially took Morse out of contention, too. Still, when the Democrats convened in Los Angeles in July, Kennedy's nomination was by no means a foregone conclusion. Both Stevenson and Johnson were potential spoilers. After meeting with Kennedy, Stevenson proclaimed neutrality. Johnson was an entirely different animal. His ambition for the presidency burned even hotter than Kennedy's.

In all respects, LBJ was the anti-JFK. Kennedy grew up in wealth and never had to worry about a dollar; Johnson grew up on a hardscrabble farm in East Texas and worked as a schoolteacher before coming to Washington as a young New Dealer in the 1930s. Kennedy was urbane and sophisticated; Johnson was crude and proud of it. At six feet three inches, he would physically intimidate his congressional colleagues when he wanted their vote or a political favor. When it came to womanizing, LBJ boasted that he'd had more women by accident than Kennedy had had on purpose.

LEFT A handbill advertises a Kennedy campaign appearance in West Virginia, 1960. Victory in that heavily Protestant state was seen by many as proof that Jack was electable despite his Catholic faith. ABOVE Jack and Jackie are greeted by a sea of supporters during a stop in New York City during the presidential campaign of 1960.

The two were different even in their similarities. Both served in the Navy in the Pacific during World War II, but Johnson somehow won a Silver Star—a medal usually awarded for valor in combat—for a single mission as an "observer" on a bombing flight. As with Kennedy, family money bankrolled Johnson's political career, but Johnson's money came from his wife, "Lady Bird" Johnson, who'd parlayed an inheritance into a lucrative radio business in Texas.

Kennedy and Johnson despised each other. In an unguarded moment, Kennedy referred to the Texan as a "fucking bastard." Johnson, always primed with inside information, knew about Kennedy's health problems, and once expressed mock indignation that Kennedy's "pediatricians" had given him a clean bill of health. In fact, the issue of Kennedy's health did surface during the campaign, but Bobby, who acted as campaign manager for his brother's campaign, successfully soft-pedaled it, denying, for example, that Kennedy suffered from Addison's disease.

As the saying goes, politics makes strange bedfellows, and Kennedy's advisers urged him to get into bed with Johnson by picking the big Texan as a running mate. Kennedy favored others for the number-two spot, but he finally gave in to his campaign advisers. Some historians believe that Kennedy

ABOVE Movie funnyman Harpo Marx campaigns for Kennedy in madcap Marx Brothers fashion, 1960.

RIGHT Memorabilia from the 1960 election. "The New Frontier" was only one of the successful slogans under which Kennedy campaigned.

A TIME FOR GREATNESS

JOHN KENNEDY
OUR NEXT PRESIDENT

LEADERSHIP *for the* **60's**

KENNEDY ★ JOHNSON

U. S. SENATOR
JOHN F.
KENNEDY
FOR
PRESIDENT

actually expected Johnson to turn down the vice-presidential offer and was somewhat taken aback when Johnson decided to sign on. After all, Johnson had tried to form an alliance with senior party members to block Kennedy's nomination in hopes of winning the top spot himself. But it would be Kennedy-Johnson in 1960. The ticket would have its advantages: Johnson was a Protestant and a southerner, and whatever his shortcomings, he was an undisputed master of the legislative process. In the Senate, he got things done—a skill that Kennedy never fully mastered.

Kennedy's acceptance speech at the Democratic convention in Los Angeles on June 15 was a masterpiece. His theme was that the nation stood on what he called a "New Frontier"—a turn of phrase that gave his campaign an inspiring and compelling catchphrase.

> *For I stand tonight facing West on what was once the last frontier. From the lands that stretch three thousand miles behind me, the pioneers of old gave up their safety, their comfort, and sometimes their own lives to build a new world here in the West. They were not the captives of their own doubts, the prisoners of their own price tags. Their motto was not "every man for himself" but "all for the common cause." They were determined to make that new world strong and free, to overcome its hazards and its hardships, to conquer the enemies that threatened from without and unknown opportunities and perils—a frontier of unknown opportunities and perils, a frontier of unfulfilled hopes and threats. . . .*
>
> *[We] stand today on the edge of a New Frontier—the frontier of the 1960s—a frontier of unfulfilled hopes and threats . . . . [I] believe the times demand new invention, innovation, imagination, decision. I am asking each of you to be pioneers on that New Frontier. My call is to the young in heart, regardless of age—to all who respond to the Scriptural call: "Be strong and of good courage; be not afraid, neither be thou dismayed."*

The highlight of the 1960 general election campaign was a series of televised debates—the first in American presidential history—between Kennedy and Nixon. On paper at least, the two were pretty evenly matched. Both were young (Nixon was just four years Kennedy's senior) and they agreed on many issues. But Nixon refused the makeup that would have concealed his perpetual five-o'clock-shadow, and his normally dour demeanor was worsened by the fact that he was in pain from a knee injury incurred a few weeks earlier. Kennedy, on the other hand, accepted the makeup and seemed to radiate confidence and charisma. Americans who listened to the debates tended to believe Nixon got the better of his opponent. Those who watched on TV believed the opposite—and in 1960, TV viewers outnumbered radio listeners.

Kennedy and his family watched the returns come in at Hyannis Port. It was a close race, and the contest was still in doubt around 3:00 a.m. when he finally went to bed. Five hours later, little Caroline bounded into his room along with her English nanny, Maud Shaw, who greeted him by saying, "Good morning, Mr. President."

RIGHT Jack and Rose at the podium at the 1960 Democratic National Convention in Los Angeles.

Kennedy had won—just. The presidential election of 1960 was the closest and most controversial chief-executive contest since Tilden vs. Hayes in 1876 and it would remain the closest until
Gore vs. Bush in 2000. Kennedy prevailed in the electoral college (303 to 219); the popular vote was
34,220,984 Kennedy to 34,108,157 Nixon—a beyond-razor-thin margin of about 0.1 percent.

Enclosures

TICKET Admission to the 1960 Democratic National Convention. It was the party's first national
convention in California in forty years, underscoring the growing population and influence of the
state—and the "Sun Belt" region in general—in American politics. BROCHURE Campaign parapher-
nalia from the 1960 race communicates the Democratic Party's growing—albeit incomplete—
support for civil rights. BALLOT In the 1960 convention, Jack won his party's nomination on the
first ballot, with 806 votes. The first runner-up, Lyndon Johnson, had only roughly half as many votes.

ABOVE Kennedy on the New York City set of the third televised presidential debate, October 13, 1960.
This was the only one of the four debates that the candidates broadcast from separate studios—Kennedy
from New York and Nixon from Hollywood. OPPOSITE Kennedy and Nixon shake hands after their second
televised debate, October 7, 1960. Nixon grasped that image-wise, Kennedy had the advantage from
the start, later writing "I never saw [Kennedy] look so fit."

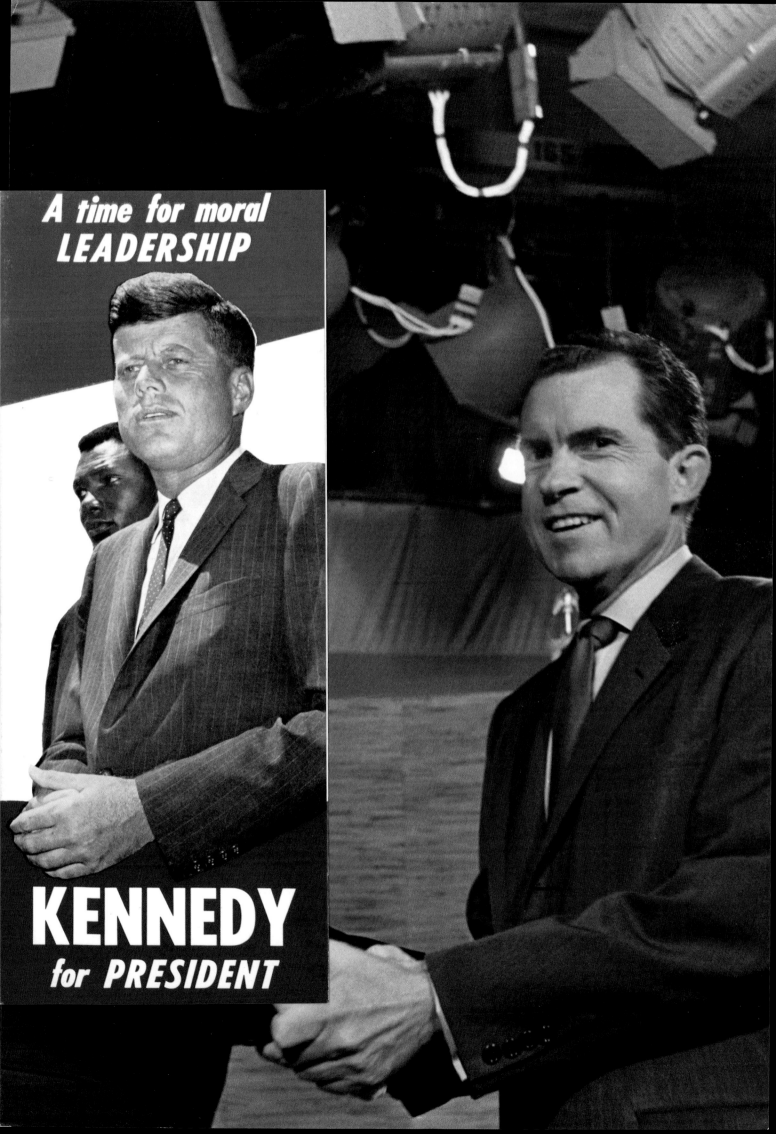

A time for moral
LEADERSHIP

KENNEDY
for PRESIDENT

In the aftermath of the election, some Republicans accused Democrats of voting fraud, especially in Illinois and Texas. Nixon would have been within his rights to demand a recount, which many of his supporters urged him to do. But he rejected the suggestion, stating that it might be "devastating" to the nation.

The president-elect and his wife appeared before the press at the local National Guard armory later that morning. "Now my wife and I prepare for a new administration—and a new baby." Fifteen days later, the new baby, John F. Kennedy Jr., arrived. For the first time since Teddy Roosevelt's presidency more than a half-century earlier, the White House would echo with the laughter and cries of young children. A new frontier indeed.

LEFT Kennedy seems to glow with health in this photo from a 1960 campaign event in Billings, Montana, but in fact, his tanned, fit look owed more to pharmaceuticals than to the sun. ABOVE Caroline kisses her new baby brother, John Jr., at Palm Beach during the transitional period following her father's victory in the 1960 general election.

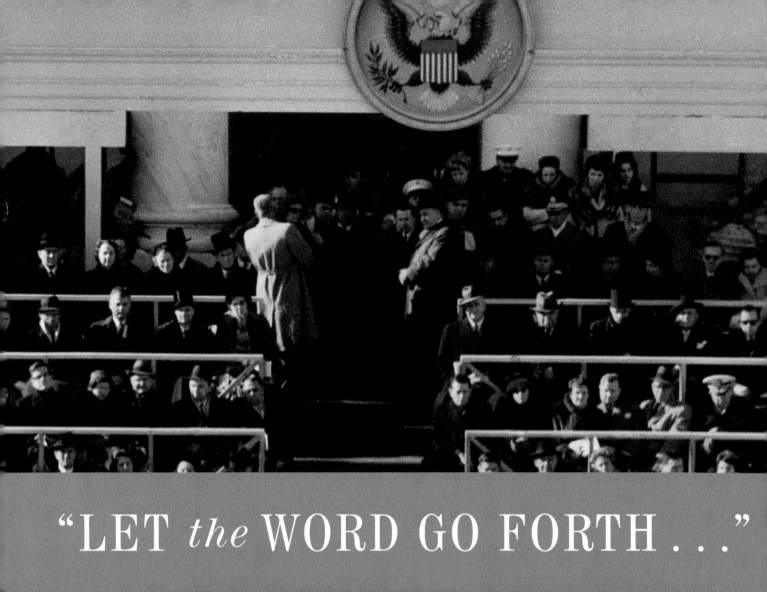

"LET *the* WORD GO FORTH . . ."

4.

was a frigid day that was nevertheless electric with anticipation. The temperature in Washington stood at 20 °F, and the snow was so deep on the streets that troops had to use flamethrowers to clear a way for the motorcade bringing the outgoing and incoming presidents and First Ladies from the White House.

President John F. Kennedy's inauguration began with the great African-American contralto Marian Anderson performing "The Star-Spangled Banner." Next, poet Robert Frost took the podium. Frost had written a new poem specifically for the occasion, but the glare of sun on the snow was too much for the elderly poet's eyes. Instead, he recited from memory the much-loved poem "The Gift Outright."

Around 1:00 p.m., Kennedy—hatless and coatless despite the cold—stepped forward and was sworn in as the thirty-fifth president of the United States by Chief Justice Earl Warren.

Kennedy's inaugural address, delivered in just under fourteen minutes, is considered the finest inaugural speech since Lincoln's two addresses. He hailed a new generation and acknowledged America's great responsibility to the rest of the world.

LEFT Hatless and coatless in the sub-freezing temperatures, Kennedy makes his renowned Inaugural Address.
ABOVE Lyndon Johnson looks on as Robert Frost recites "The Gift Outright" at Kennedy's Inauguration.

Let the word go forth from this time and place, to friend and foe alike, that the torch has been passed to a new generation of Americans—born in this century, tempered by war, disciplined by a hard and bitter peace, proud of our ancient heritage—and unwilling to witness or permit the slow undoing of those human rights to which this nation has always been committed, and to which we are committed today at home and around the world. . . .

Let every nation know, whether it wishes us well or ill, that we shall pay any price, bear any burden, meet any hardship, support any friend, oppose any foe, to assure the survival and the success of liberty. . . . In the long history of the world, only a few generations have been granted the role of defending freedom in its hour of maximum danger. I do not shrink from this responsibility—I welcome it. I do not believe that any of us would exchange places with any other people or any other generation. The energy, the faith, the devotion which we bring to this endeavor will light our country and all who serve it—and the glow from that fire can truly light the world.

And so, my fellow Americans: Ask not what your country can do for you—ask what you can do for your country.

ABOVE This photograph beautifully captures the drama and power of the Inauguration. RIGHT The famous state dinner for Nobel Prize winners, April 29, 1962. Among the American "Nobelists" were chemist Glenn Seaborg and writers Pearl S. Buck and Ernest Hemingway.

More than a million people cheered the new president as he returned to the White House to review the inaugural parade. That night there were no fewer than five inaugural balls. Jackie, tired, returned to the White House early. An elated Jack stayed out until 3:00 a.m., winding up at a private party at journalist Joe Alsop's house in Georgetown.

It was a glittering start to a glittering new era for the White House, one in which high culture and the arts played a major role for the first time in American history. The Kennedys' predecessors, the Eisenhowers and the Trumans, were people of plain tastes, and their styles of entertaining reflected this. State dinners for distinguished guests were usually staid, ordinary affairs. The Kennedys aimed for something far more sophisticated. State dinners and other White House social events would now feature formal dress, fine wines, and exquisite cuisine prepared by a French-trained chef.

Guests at these events and at more intimate dinners and parties included not only foreign and domestic dignitaries, but people accomplished in a variety of fields—cellist Pablo Casals, scientists J. Robert Oppenheimer and Linus Pauling, and composer Igor Stravinsky. The best-remembered state dinner of the Kennedy years took place on April 29, 1962, for forty-nine Nobel Prize winners and one hundred and twenty-six other guests. Kennedy told the diners, "[This is] the most extraordinary collection of talent, of human knowledge, that has ever been gathered together in the White House, with the possible exception of when Thomas Jefferson dined alone."

The White House was soon transformed physically, too, by Jackie's doing. When she arrived, the executive mansion's interior was a dowdy mess of mismatched furniture and décor. In February 1961, she formed a commission that included interior decorators, antiques experts, and art historians, and set about a complete restoration. As she told *Time* magazine, "Everything in the White House must have a reason for being there. It would be sacrilege merely to 'redecorate' it—a word I hate. It must be restored—and that has nothing to do with decoration. That is a question of scholarship."

She appealed to owners of period furniture to contribute pieces to the White House, imported others, and tracked down artworks and artifacts from previous administrations that had disappeared into museums and warehouses. To fund the endeavor, she wrote a guidebook to the White House that sold a half-million copies. Jackie showed off the stunning results by taking the nation on a televised tour of the White House (featuring a cameo by the new president). Aired on CBS on February 14, 1962, and rebroadcast on NBC three nights later, the program was seen by three out of four American TV viewers.

Inevitably, there was some criticism of this new high style, of the fact that Jackie preferred French to American designers for her dresses, and the fact that menu cards were printed in French. But the majority of Americans saw the new look of the White House and the family that lived in it as a source of pride.

Enclosures

MENU The dishes for the Nobel Prize dinner were prepared by French chef René Verdon and paired with appropriate wines—also French. DRAFT Kennedy's handwritten excerpts from his Inaugural Address. Kennedy and Ted Sorensen began work on the speech while flying from Palm Beach to Washington on January 17, 1961, just three days before the Inauguration.

ABOVE The Red Room—one of three state parlors on the first floor of the White House—was among the first parts of the Executive Mansion restored by the First Lady. The American Empire–style furniture was uphol-stered in red cerise silk to match the color of the walls. RIGHT Jack and Jackie at a Christmas party for the White House staff, 1962. As writer and White House guest William Styron put it, "Jack and Jackie actually shimmered. . . . They were truly the golden couple."

Jackie also made the mansion's family quarters in the East Wing more family-friendly, adding a kitchen and rooms for Caroline and John Jr. Deeply concerned with preserving her children's privacy, she organized a kind of kindergarten within the White House for Caroline and a carefully selected group of children. Jack was a loving, doting father. He found his offspring a source of comfort and a refuge from the stress of the nation's toughest job, and he spent as much time with them as he could. Visitors to the Oval Office would find the president playing hide-and-seek with John Jr. around his desk or sitting in his rocking chair with both kids on his lap.

Whenever possible, Jack would break away from business to say goodnight to Caroline and John Jr. when they were put to bed. When the president was finally ready to retire himself, Jackie told journalist Theodore H. White shortly after Jack's death, he liked to end the day by listening to the final song from the Lerner & Loewe musical *Camelot*, in which King Arthur remembers the glory days of his court:

Don't let it be forgot

That once there was a spot

For one brief shining moment that was known

As Camelot

Over the years, the term "Camelot" became enshrined in America's collective memory as a metaphor for the Kennedy White House.

ABOVE Jack claps while Caroline and John Jr. dance in the Oval Office. RIGHT Father and son stroll on the White House's West Wing Colonnade. The public came to know John Jr. as "John-John," but the Kennedys themselves were never heard to call him that.

A SHAKY START

Kennedy brought his trusted crew with him to the White House, including secretary Evelyn Lincoln, special assistants Kenny O'Donnell and Dave Powers, and the man the president described as "my intellectual blood bank," Ted Sorensen. For the top jobs in his cabinet, Kennedy tapped experienced diplomat Dean Rusk as secretary of state; the secretary of defense slot ultimately went to Robert S. McNamara, a Ford Motor Company executive renowned for his computer-like mind; and C. Douglas Dillon, a businessman who'd served as undersecretary of state in the Eisenhower administration, was appointed to the Treasury. Kennedy originally offered the post of attorney general to Connecticut senator Abraham Ribicoff, but at his father's insistence, it went to Bobby—an appointment that wasn't without controversy, for the obvious reason that people would object to nepotism.

Jack would come to rely heavily on his brother's judgment and energy: "If I want something done and done immediately I rely on the attorney general. He is very much the doer in this administration, and has an organizational gift I have rarely if ever seen surpassed." Bobby used the Justice Department's powers to vigorously uphold existing civil-rights laws, and privately he advised his brother to go further in supporting the struggle against discrimination and for equality at the polls. During the

TOP LEFT The president takes some time off from the world's toughest job to play with John Jr. BOTTOM LEFT Jack leads Caroline and her pony, Macaroni. ABOVE Kennedy and Johnson confer in the Oval Office.

presidential campaign, for example, it had been Bobby who persuaded Jack to make a phone call to Coretta Scott King, whose husband, civil-rights leader Martin Luther King Jr., was in jail in Birmingham, Alabama.

Bobby's other big project was going after organized crime and its influence on labor unions; his tenacity (organized-crime convictions rose 800 percent on his watch) earned him the enmity of mob leaders and corrupt union officials such as the Teamster president Jimmy Hoffa.

The new administration's odd man out was the vice president. He despised the Kennedy crowd (Bobby especially) as a bunch of effete east coast intellectuals. The loathing was mutual; members of the Kennedy inner circle reportedly nicknamed the VP "Uncle Cornpone." Johnson also missed the power he'd wielded as Senate majority leader. He dutifully did what he was told to do and went where he was told to go, but he made no secret of his dissatisfaction with his role as number two in command.

At first, foreign affairs preoccupied the incoming administration. Around the world, "flash points" threatened to ignite the Cold War into hot war. These included Berlin, Southeast Asia, and—just ninety miles from American shores—Cuba.

A revolution led by Fidel Castro had overthrown the dictatorial government of President Fulgencio Batista in 1959. Not long afterward, Castro declared himself a "Marxist-Leninist" and allied the island nation with the Soviet Union, to the consternation of the United States. Not only was it an

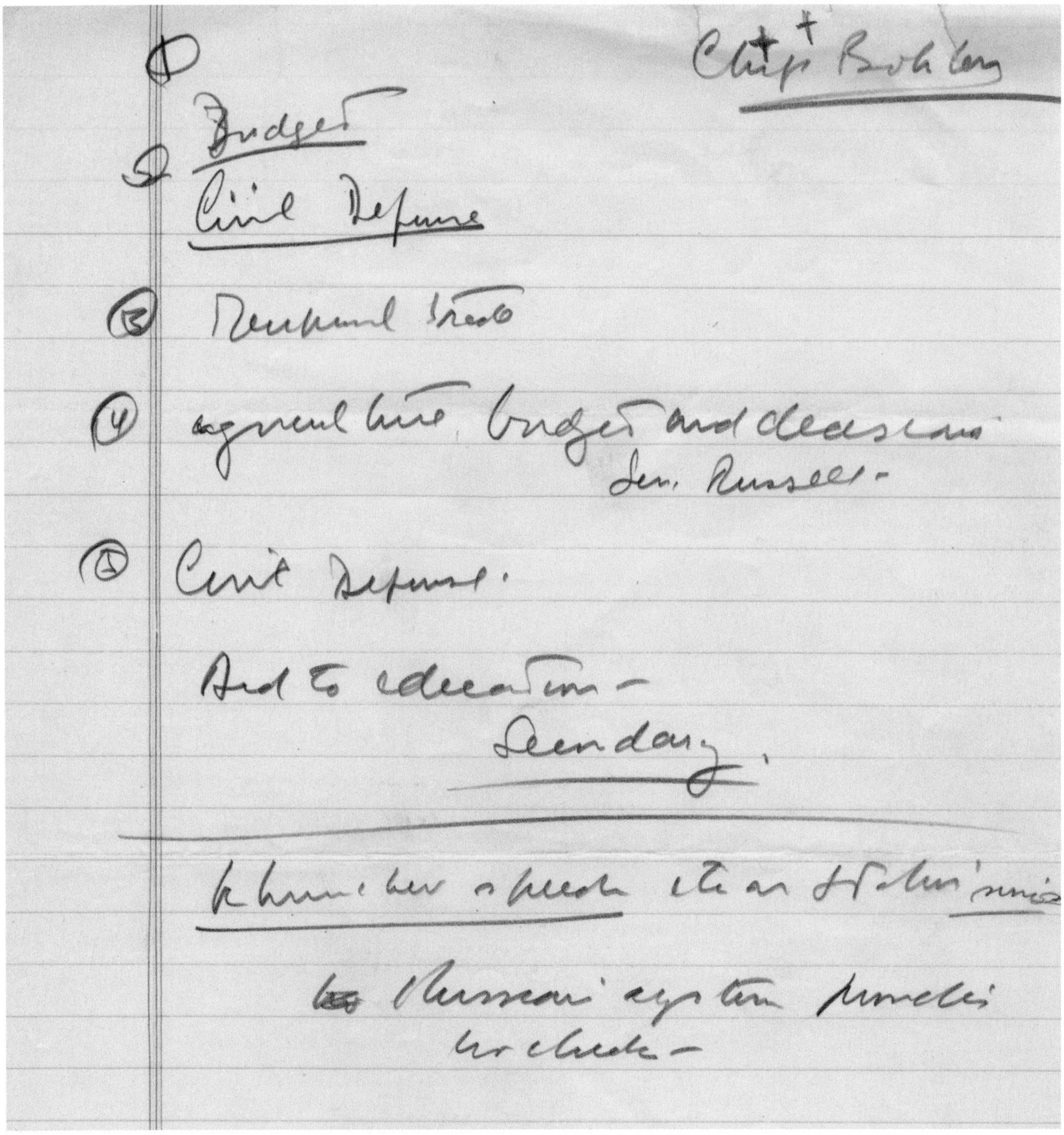

[Handwritten notes, largely illegible. Partially readable items include:]

Chip's Bohlen †

1. Budget
2. Civil Defense
3. [illegible]
4. agriculture, budget and decisions
   Sen. Russell –
5. Civil Defense.

   Aid to education –
   Secondary.

embarrassment to have a Soviet client state in America's backyard, many feared that if Castro stayed in power, he'd export Soviet-style communism throughout Latin America, where several nations were already facing left-wing insurgencies.

Cuba was an important point on Kennedy's foreign policy agenda. During the election campaign, he had criticized President Eisenhower for not doing enough about Castro. Having successfully overthrown leftist governments in Iran and Guatemala in the 1950s, the outgoing Eisenhower administration did have a plan for Cuba. Kennedy was briefed on it over Thanksgiving 1960. The plan, developed by the CIA, involved arming and training a force of anti-Castro Cuban exiles in Guatemala. From there they'd infiltrate the island and attempt to spark a popular uprising.

Once in the White House, Kennedy gave the go-ahead, and the date for the operation was set for mid-April. Even so, Kennedy was concerned about the size of the force that would be needed for

LEFT Kennedy, members of his cabinet, and advisers meet at Hyannis Port. Jack liked to hold these vacation cabinet meetings in the morning so he could spend the afternoons sailing aboard the Kennedy family yacht, the *Honey Fitz*. ABOVE Kennedy's notes on military planning and civil defense, April 1961. The president's handwriting was so bad many had trouble reading his notes and drafts.

the operation. Reportedly, he said, "It sounds like D-Day." He also worried about the location of the proposed landing, which changed late in the development of the plans and meant that the landing troops would be cut off from native rebels in the mountains who could aid in the uprising. Some of his advisers, including Dean Rusk, urged him to cancel. The obstacles were huge. There was really no way to disguise U.S. involvement. News of the operation might leak to the press, scuttling the element of surprise needed if the operation was to have any chance of success. Also, there was the problem of air cover. The invasion force—"Brigade 2506"—had only a few World War II–surplus planes supplied by the CIA. The Cuban air force was tiny too, but it had jets. Despite these hindrances, Jack remained firm, telling retractors, "I'm not going to chicken out."

The invasion began on April 17, 1961. Preinvasion airstrikes on Cuban airfields failed to destroy all the government's military aircraft, so Kennedy finally permitted two fighters from a U.S. Navy carrier to protect Brigade 2506's aircraft. They arrived over the landing zone at Cuba's *Bahía de Cochinos* (the Bay of Pigs) too late. The invaders also hoped their arrival would spark a popular anti-Castro uprising; it never materialized. Cuban forces quickly isolated the area. The invaders who got ashore were captured or killed.

The failure of the Bay of Pigs operation was a serious blow to the new president. By allowing the operation to go ahead, he appeared reckless; by not providing more support, he looked weak. Beside the damage to his image and his administration's credibility at home and abroad, it hit him hard personally. He knew what it was like to lose men in combat and he cried when he learned the fate of Brigade 2506. Later, Kennedy would face the survivors in person when Castro released them in return

for American medical supplies. At an emotional event at Miami's Orange Bowl on December 29, 1962, the anti-Castro fighters presented Kennedy with their unit flag. "I can assure you," he told them, "that this flag will be returned to this brigade in a free Havana. "

The CIA continued its efforts to undermine the Cuban government. These efforts didn't exclude assassination attempts against Castro himself. In fact, plans for Castro's elimination may have been in place even before the Bay of Pigs, and it may have been CIA assurances that Castro would be dead before the exiles hit the beach that influenced Kennedy's decision to green-light the operation. The CIA's anti-Castro program, code-named Operation Mongoose, bordered on the farcical. Plans included plots to blow up Castro by planting an exploding seashell off a beach where he liked to swim and spiking his food with female hormones to make his trademark bushy beard fall out.

LEFT Managing smiles at a somber event, Jack and Jackie meet with the survivors of the Bay of Pigs invasion force at Miami's Orange Bowl stadium on December 29, 1962. ABOVE The survivors present the president with their brigade flag.

Kennedy's first overseas trip as president came not long after the Bay of Pigs. By this point, his

medical condition was a closely monitored aspect of his everyday routine and his travel regimen.

In May, he and Jackie flew to Paris to meet with French president Charles de Gaulle, followed by a

summit meeting in Vienna with Soviet premier Nikita Khrushchev. Kennedy's rocking chair and the

horsehide mattress that eased his back went with him aboard Air Force One. Another passenger was

Dr. Max Jacobson, nicknamed "Dr. Feelgood," whose celebrity clients ranged from writers Tennessee

Williams and Truman Capote to movie director Cecil B. DeMille. Jacobson's specialty was administer-

ing a mysterious mix of drugs via injection—later determined to be mostly amphetamine, a.k.a. speed.

Kennedy had first received Jacobson's "treatment" during the 1960 campaign. After throwing out

his back during a tree-planting ceremony the following spring, Jack invited Jacobson for the first of

what would be many visits to the White House—much to the consternation of his official physicians,

ABOVE French President Charles de Gaulle greets Jack during the Paris stopover en route to the Vienna

summit with Nikita Khrushchev, June 1961. RIGHT Excerpts from the "Order of the Day" for June 3 and 4,

1961, are detailed to the minute and down to the dress code.

June 2, 1961

PRESIDENT'S MEETING WITH CHAIRMAN KHRUSHCHEV

JUNE 3 - JUNE 4, 1961

ORDER OF THE DAY
Saturday, June 3

8:15 a.m.	The President and Mrs. Kennedy, accompanied by the Secretary, depart from the Quai d'Orsay for Orly Field. The Prime Minister and Mme. Debre will attend the President and Mrs. Kennedy. Foreign Minister Couve de Murville will attend the Secretary.
8:45 a.m.	The President and Mrs. Kennedy and the Secretary arrive at Orly Field. No departure ceremony.
9:00 a.m.	Airborne for Vienna.
10:40 a.m.	The President and Mrs. Kennedy and the Secretary arrive at Schwechat Airport, Vienna. Airport arrival ceremony. Receiving line: President Schaerf, Chancellor Gorbach, Vice Chancellor Pittermann, Foreign Minister Kreisky and others. Brief word of welcome from President Schaerf with brief response from the President. National anthems. Walk by Honor Guard from apron to car assembly point outside airport. Dress: Dark suit.
11:00 a.m.	Departure from Schwechat Airport.
12:00 Noon	The President and the Secretary arrive at the Embassy Residence.
12:45 p.m.	Chairman Khrushchev arrives at the Embassy Residence.
12:45 p.m. - 1:30 p.m.	The President meets with Chairman Khrushchev.
1:00 p.m. - 3:00 p.m.	The President hosts a luncheon for Chairman Khrushchev at the Embassy Residence.

Participants:

United States	Soviet Union
The President	(to be determined)
The Secretary	
Ambassador Mathews	
Mr. Bundy	
Ambassador Thompson	
Mr. Bohlen	
Mr. Kohler	
Mr. Nitze	
Mr. Armitage	
Mr. Akalovsky (Interpreter)	

3:00 p.m. - 6:00 p.m.	The President meets with Chairman Khrushchev at the Embassy Residence.

the Secret Service, the FBI, and Bobby, all of whom worried about just what "Dr. Feelgood" was inject-

ing into the president. Kennedy found that Jacobson's injections not only eased his constant pain but

made him feel (in Jacobson's words) "cool, calm, and very alert." "I don't care if it's horse piss," Jack

told Bobby, "it works." Wanting to be at the top of his game in what would clearly be a crucial encoun-

ter with Khrushchev, Kennedy decided to take Jacobson and his medical bag to Europe.

In Paris, Jackie received a rapturous reception from the French public. The *très chic* First Lady even

succeeded in charming the famously haughty de Gaulle. Jackie's popularity prompted Jack to famously

declare, "I am the man who accompanied Jacqueline Kennedy to Paris, and I have enjoyed it."

At his next stop in Vienna, there were three major items on the table: nuclear disarmament, especially

Kennedy's desire for an international ban on further testing of nuclear weapons; Laos, the former

French colony in Southeast Asia where Soviet guerillas, the Pathet Lao, threatened the government; and

Berlin, where tensions were high in a city uneasily divided between Western and Soviet zones of control.

The summit with Khrushchev began badly and didn't improve. For the first couple of days, the

tough, earthy Soviet leader wagged his finger in the president's face and lectured on the superiority

of the communist system while repeating his determination to help spread it around the world.

Khrushchev brushed off Kennedy's nuclear test-ban proposal. There was some compromise over Laos. But president and premier remained at loggerheads over Berlin.

During World War II, a "four-power agreement" between Britain, France, the Soviet Union, and the United States called for the division of Germany into four occupation zones, each to be administered by one of the allied nations. After the onset of the Cold War, the Western allies merged their zones into an independent nation, the Federal Republic of Germany (West Germany) while the Soviet zone became a Soviet client state—the German Democratic Republic (East Germany). The city of Berlin, though located deep inside East Germany, remained divided into Western and Soviet zones.

West Berlin was, in essence, an island of freedom in a Soviet-dominated sea. This scenario was problematic for Khrushchev and East German premier Walter Ulbricht. Dissatisfied with life under communism, tens of thousands of East Germans traveled to East Berlin, where they could cross over to West Berlin simply by taking a subway or streetcar. Because the World War II–era agreement

LEFT President de Gaulle escorts Mrs. Kennedy to dinner at the Palace of Versailles, June 1961. ABOVE Not even the dour Soviet premier was immune to Jackie's charms.

guaranteed free access to Berlin by road, rail, and air, these refugees could then reach West Germany

and begin new lives.

Ulbricht and Khrushchev were desperate to stem the tide of refugees to the West. Khrushchev threat-

ened to sign a treaty with East Germany that would block Western access to Berlin. There was no way

Kennedy could accept this. He knew that allowing such an agreement would send a signal to America's

European allies—and the wider world—that the United States would not stand by its commitments.

The Kennedy–Khrushchev talks ended with the premier telling the president that "It was up to

the United States to decide whether there will be war or peace. The Soviet Union will sign [the treaty]

in December."

"Then, Mr. Chairman, there will be war," Jack shot back. "It will be a cold winter."

Kennedy returned to Washington feeling humiliated by Khrushchev. He told an aide, "He treated me like a little boy!" He was also pessimistic about the chances of preserving peace. At that time, Berlin was the brightest of countless Cold War flash points. Following World War II, the old European empires in Africa and Asia had crumbled. Scores of new nations had come into being—some peacefully, others through armed struggle against their former colonial overlords. The West, led by the United States, now found itself in fierce competition with the Soviet Union for the loyalty of these nonaligned nations. This competition was the crux of the Cold War, and it was pushing the two nations to amass larger and larger arsenals.

Kennedy pressed Congress for funding for a general military buildup and an increase in the number of intercontinental ballistic missiles (ICBMs) and more nuclear-powered submarines to deliver them. He also promoted a nationwide civil defense program in case the unthinkable—a nuclear

LEFT Kennedy and Khrushchev conversing in Vienna. ABOVE The President greets Peace Corps volunteers on the White House's South Lawn, August 28, 1961.

war—came to pass. "Duck and cover" drills, in which schoolchildren were taught to hide under their desks at the sight of an atomic flash, would become part of the collective memory of the "baby boom" generation. Some of their parents dug backyard "fallout shelters" stocked with supplies.

As part of the new president's pledge to "pay any price, bear any burden, meet any hardship, support any friend, oppose any foe, to assure the survival and the success of liberty," the United States increased military support, both openly and secretly, for nations battling left-wing insurgencies.

Jack recognized that the United States had to do something beyond sending teams of U.S. Army Special Forces (specifically authorized by the president to wear green berets) or dispatching CIA operatives into postcolonial trouble spots. In the spring of 1961, he established a new federal agency, the Peace Corps, "to promote world peace and friendship [by making] available to interested countries and areas men and women of the United States qualified for service abroad and willing to serve, under conditions of hardship if necessary, to help the peoples of such countries and areas in meeting their needs for trained manpower."

Once again keeping things in the family, Jack appointed his brother-in-law, Sargent Shriver (his sister Eunice's husband) as the Corps' first director. Over the next five years, some 15,000 Americans—mostly young people just out of high school or college—served stints in more than fifty countries. From Afghanistan to Uruguay, Peace Corps volunteers helped local populations improve agriculture, health care, infrastructure, and education.

Kennedy also recognized the need to improve America's image among its Latin American neighbors—an image tarnished by often heavy-handed foreign policy and occasional military interventions. In August 1961, he announced the Alliance for Progress, an ambitious ten-year program aimed at increasing economic growth, promoting literacy, and fostering land reform in the region. The program had some success in its early years, though it would go into decline after Kennedy's death.

"NOT BECAUSE IT IS EASY, BUT BECAUSE IT IS HARD . . ."

Kennedy's early presidential initiatives reached beyond the scope of any previous president's foreign policy activities. In the spring of 1961, the new president extended "the New Frontier" into space. On April 12, as the tragedy of the Bay of Pigs was just unfolding, Soviet cosmonaut Yuri Gagarin became the first human being in space in an orbital mission. It was a huge propaganda coup for the Soviets. Kennedy observed the worldwide joy at Gagarin's achievement with dismay. On April 14, he called in various advisers and asked, "What can we do now? . . . Can we put a man on the moon before them?" As a senator and in his first months in the White House, Kennedy had been largely uninterested in manned space exploration. The enormous sums of money required could be better spent on domestic concerns, he felt, and he held the view that unmanned probes could do whatever manned missions

LEFT Kennedy with R. Sargent Shriver, presidential brother-in-law and first director of the Peace Corps.

could do. But now, Kennedy saw the space race as another element in America's endeavor to beat out the Soviet Union.

The Soviets had already defeated the United States with the launch of the first satellite and the first manned space flight. Going to the moon was indeed the only way to win the space race. Kennedy tasked Lyndon Johnson with analyzing the situation, and he endorsed Johnson's conclusion that "In the eyes of the world, first in space means first, period; second in space means second in everything." The final winner of the space race would be the first nation to put a man on the moon. Kennedy's new-found interest in space was bolstered a couple of weeks later when astronaut Alan Shepard became the first American in space. Shepard's mission, however, was suborbital and only lasted fifteen minutes.

On May 25, Jack made his case before a joint session of Congress, stating, "I believe we should go to the moon." He repeated this contention in a speech at Rice University the following year:

> We choose to go to the moon in this decade and do the other things, not because they are easy, but because they are hard, because that goal will serve to organize and measure the best of our energies and skills, because that challenge is one that we are willing to accept, one we are unwilling to postpone, and one which we intend to win, and the others, too.
>
> It is for these reasons that I regard the decision last year to shift our efforts in space from low to high gear as among the most important decisions that will be made during my incumbency in the office of the Presidency.

Within a couple of years, more than 200,000 people were at work on the Apollo program, which encompassed the "moon shot" and associated missions, and the budget of NASA (the National Aeronautics and Space Administration) had tripled. Sadly, the goal would be achieved after Kennedy's death. On July 20, 1969, Neil Armstrong stepped off the ladder of *Apollo II*'s lunar module and touched down on the moon—beating the Soviets.

Kennedy may have kicked the space race into high gear as a way of one-upping the Soviets, but he saw the benefits of cooperation as well as competition. Twice during his presidency, he contacted Khrushchev about pooling American and Soviet resources in space exploration. Khrushchev was receptive, but Kennedy's assassination ended further talk of U.S.–Soviet cooperation in space until the 1970s.

Enclosures

LETTER A note from Khrushchev to Kennedy following *Mercury* astronaut Gordon Cooper's space flight on May 15, 1963. The Soviet premier could easily be magnanimous in his congratulations to Kennedy because the USSR still held a strong lead in the space race. TELEGRAM Correspondence from the U.S. State Department, acknowledging the congratulations offered by Khrushchev. DOODLES Kennedy's page of notes from a meeting about the Bay of Pigs.

RIGHT Jack and Jackie watch the televised broadcast of Alan Shepard becoming the first astronaut in space.

LEADER *of the* FREE WORLD

MRBM FIELD LAUNCH SITE
SAN CRISTOBAL NO 2
14 OCTOBER 1962

EQUIPMENT

TENTS

CONVOY

6 MISSILE TRAILERS

TENTS

5.

of the Kennedy presidency—one that threatened to plunge the United States and the Soviet Union into nuclear war—began as Kennedy tucked into his usual bacon-and-eggs breakfast on the morning of October 16, 1962. His national security adviser McGeorge Bundy presented him with a sheaf of photographs taken from a spy plane flying high over Cuba. They showed that the Soviet Union had installed nuclear missiles on the island. Analysts determined that they were intermediate-range ballistic missiles (IRBMs) with sufficient range to reach Washington. Thinking that he'd taken the measure of Kennedy at Vienna the previous year, Khrushchev had gambled on putting missiles in Cuba to counter the overall U.S. superiority in nuclear weapons, especially submarine-launched missiles.

Kennedy convened an emergency meeting of EXCOMM (the Executive Committee on National Defense), which included Bobby and the Joint Chiefs of Staff. The military men urged an immediate bombing of the missile launch sites followed by an invasion of Cuba. Kennedy demurred. Beyond the inherent risks, he believed that Khrushchev would use an attack on Cuba to occupy West Berlin.

LEFT The strain on Kennedy shows plainly in this photo taken during the Cuban Missile Crisis. ABOVE Photographs from high-flying U-2 spy planes pinpointed Soviet missile launch sites in Cuba.

But something had to be done. If the Soviets managed to get medium-range ballistic missiles (MRBMs, with a much longer range than IRBMs) into Cuba, ninety percent of the continental United States would be under threat of the mushroom cloud. Jack ultimately decided that the best tactic would be a naval blockade of Cuba, with U.S. warships inspecting all Cuba-bound vessels and turning around any with military hardware.

The public learned of the crisis on the evening of October 22 when Jack addressed the nation, stating that "This secret, swift, and extraordinary buildup of communist missiles [is] deliberately provocative and unjustified. . . . Aggressive conduct, if allowed to go unchecked, ultimately leads to war." Millions of Americans wondered if they should have dug that backyard fallout shelter after all.

The naval blockade (officially referred to by the less warlike term "quarantine") began the following morning. A convoy of Soviet merchant ships, escorted by submarines, was then steaming toward the quarantine line set five hundred miles off the Cuban coast.

ABOVE **EXCOMM** in conference during the missile crisis. RIGHT Bobby was Jack's closest confidant during the crisis as he was so many other times. His advice helped steel Jack to resist his military chiefs' urging of a preemptive air strike on Cuba.

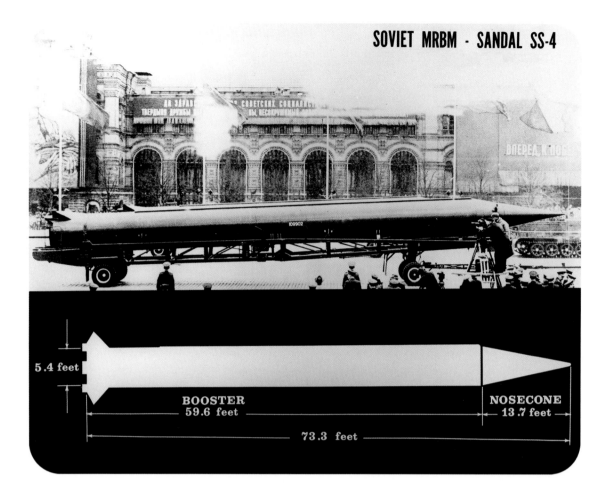

SOVIET MRBM · SANDAL SS-4

5.4 feet

BOOSTER
59.6 feet

NOSECONE
13.7 feet

73.3 feet

Later that day, the Soviet vessels turned around. "We are eyeball to eyeball," Secretary of State Dean Rusk exclaimed, "and I think the other fellow just blinked." But the crisis was far from over. The United States still had to persuade the Soviets to remove the existing missiles from Cuba. The Joint Chiefs of Staff still favored bombing the missile site and possibly invading Cuba. Kennedy had threatened to retaliate if any American spy planes were shot down over Cuba. But when antiaircraft fire downed a U-2 aircraft, killing its pilot, Kennedy decided against launching an air strike.

Meanwhile, secret communications between the United States, the Soviets, and their respective allies went on at a fevered pace, including a series of personal messages between Kennedy and Khrushchev. The Soviet leader laid his cards on the table: He wanted a guarantee that the United States wouldn't invade Cuba, and he wanted American Jupiter nuclear missiles removed from Turkey. Kennedy agreed to both conditions. It wasn't much of a concession; the Jupiters were obsolete and due to be withdrawn anyway. But Kennedy didn't want to be seen as giving too much to the Soviets in the bargain, and he saw to it that the removal of the Jupiters remained secret.

The world had been poised on a nuclear knife-edge for two weeks when Khrushchev announced that the Soviet missiles would be removed from Cuba. "In order to save the world, we have to retreat," he told the Politburo (the Soviet parliament). The Cuban Missile Crisis was over. The world breathed a collective sigh of relief. Kennedy might not have been much of a poker player, but he'd played this

LEFT The president takes questions at a press conference during the missile crisis. ABOVE A photo of a Soviet medium-range ballistic missile (MRBM), probably taken secretly during the annual May Day parade in Moscow and smuggled to the West.

minimum

24 hours medium

minimum Continuing

Missile

Missile

Missile

veto

Close surveillance

veto

warned

veto

veto

veto

Maneuvering

Scribbled notes during meeting of Security Council Oct 25, 1962

Provocative

nuclear shares

Buchanan

Diplomatic

Soviet ship

Passenger interest

Barnes

Barnes

Camouflage

Cody

Grozny

Pengelly

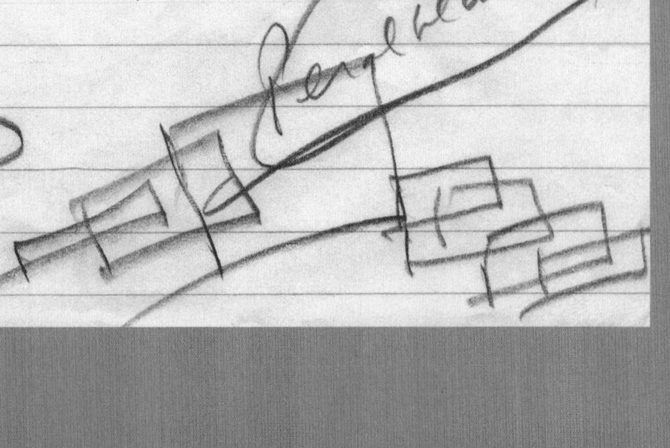

particular hand with consummate skill—and the stakes couldn't have been higher. His attitude was typically ironic: "Nobody wants to go through what we went through in Cuba very often."

WE SHALL OVERCOME

While Kennedy faced down Khrushchev and urged the nation to shoot for the moon, millions of African Americans were still struggling to exercise their right to vote, to eat lunch, watch a movie, or drink from a water fountain without being confronted by a "Whites Only" sign. They desired lives free of discrimination and intimidation.

The civil rights movement brought African Americans and their white supporters together for organized "sit-ins" to integrate restaurants and other facilities, staged "freedom rides" aboard buses to test the law forbidding segregation in interstate transportation, and attempted to take their places at formerly segregated schools and universities throughout the South. They met resistance—often violent—from local mobs, police, and high officials alike.

Kennedy had always broadly supported civil rights, but he favored a limited, gradual approach. This was mostly a political stance. In the early 1960s, the South was still the "Solid South," which meant it was overwhelmingly Democratic. Pushing too hard on civil rights would alienate conservative

LEFT Presidential notes and doodles, made during an EXCOMM meeting. ABOVE Pages from secretary Evelyn Lincoln's daybook show Jack's packed schedule of meetings from October 20 through October 22, 1962.

Democratic Southerners in the state houses and in Congress and undercut the president's support in his own party, while Southern politicians constantly cried that any attempts by Washington to guarantee voting rights and promote integration amounted to unconstitutional violations of states' rights.

African-American leaders like Martin Luther King Jr., however, were insistent that this soft approach to the civil rights question wasn't making a difference. And Kennedy was well aware that the situation in the South was doing great harm to America's image abroad. The president's commitment to promoting freedom around the world looked hypocritical when police turned fire hoses and attack dogs on nonviolent protestors at home. Kennedy said that the images "made him sick."

At first, Kennedy focused on enforcing existing civil-rights laws rather than proposing new ones. In September 1962, he sent federal marshals to the University of Mississippi when a white mob took over the campus in an attempt to keep an African-American veteran, James Meredith, from enrolling. The situation escalated into a riot that claimed two lives, and Kennedy sent in federal troops and U.S. Marshals.

Stirred into action by the University of Mississippi episode, Jack submitted a moderate civil rights bill to Congress early in 1963. But in the teeth of Southern opposition, it went nowhere. That spring, two African-American students attempted to enroll at the University of Alabama. The state's ultra-segregationist governor, George Wallace, stood in the door of the school's auditorium to physically bar their entrance. The result was a tense standoff, and again, federal authorities had to be sent in.

ABOVE Alabama governor George Wallace literally stands in the door to halt desegregation of the state university. RIGHT The Rev. Martin Luther King Jr. meets with Lyndon Johnson at the White House.

On the night of June 11, Kennedy appeared on TV to speak on civil rights: "This is not a sectional issue, nor is this a partisan issue. . . . We are confronted by a moral issue. It is as old as the Scriptures and is as clear as the American Constitution. . . . We face, therefore, a moral crisis as a country and as a people." He backed up his words by sending a beefed-up civil rights bill to Congress later that month. This one called for a federal guarantee of voting rights and a dismantling of the segregation system that had made African Americans second-class citizens in their own country since the 1890s. Once again, the bill languished. However, it would form the basis of the Civil Rights Act that would eventually pass the House and Senate the following year.

The 1964 Civil Rights Act was a landmark piece of legislation, and it was undoubtedly a product of Kennedy's efforts. The bill outlawed racial segregation in schools, public places, and employment. It prohibited discrimination in public facilities, in government, and in employment, creating the Equal Employment Opportunity Commission. Though Kennedy would not live to see the bill's passage, he would be hailed for his great conviction and early work towards equality.

Enclosures

LETTER The president's message to Mississippi governor Ross Barnett demanding that Barnett indicate whether or not he intended to continue to fight enforcement of federal civil rights law.
PRESIDENTIAL STATEMENT Kennedy issued this official response to the bombing of civil rights activists' houses in Birmingham, Alabama.

ABOVE Following Martin Luther King Jr.'s speech at the Lincoln Memorial, Kennedy invited him and other civil-rights leaders to the White House, where he assured them he intended to press more fully for civil rights legislation. RIGHT A quarter of a million people—many more than expected—came to Washington to hear not only King, but also other civil rights leaders, such as A. Philip Randolph and Whitney Young Jr., and musicians, such as Marian Anderson, Odetta, and Bob Dylan.

"LET THEM COME TO BERLIN"

Kennedy had never given up his hope of negotiating an agreement that would halt, or at least limit, further testing of nuclear weapons. As the father of young children, the issue was personal as well as political. "I know this sounds corny," he told Undersecretary of State Chester Bowles, "but our world doesn't matter very much. Caroline's world does matter, and I'm prepared to take every conceivable step to bring about a nuclear agreement with Russia."

Khrushchev felt that such a treaty could only favor the West. The Soviet premier also continued to doubt the American president's sincerity.

On June 10, Kennedy addressed the graduating class at Washington's American University, urging them—and the nation—to "re-examine our attitude toward the Soviet Union. . . . In the final analysis our most basic common link is that we all inhabit this small planet," he went on. "We all breathe the same air. We all cherish our children. And we are all mortal." Peace between the West and the Communist bloc had to be "the necessary and rational end of rational men." If other nations halted testing of nuclear weapons in the earth's atmosphere, Kennedy promised, the United States would do the same.

It was a politically risky move. Most of the president's military advisers were against any limits on testing, and there were plenty of hard-liners in Congress—in both parties—who believed that *any* agreement with the Soviets was tantamount to sending up a white flag in the Cold War.

But Kennedy had an ally in British Prime Minister Harold Macmillan and an astute liaison to the Soviets in the veteran diplomat Averell Harriman. Kennedy's "peace speech" had broken the ice with Khrushchev, who described it as "the best statement by any president since [Franklin] Roosevelt." Harriman went to Moscow and Kennedy worked on a draft treaty. The process was facilitated by the "hot line," a direct communications link between the White House and the Kremlin set up in the wake of the Cuban Missile Crisis.

While negotiations went on, Kennedy made another trip to Europe. His main objective was to show American support for the people of West Berlin. In August 1961, not long after the chilly Vienna summit meeting between Kennedy and Khrushchev, the East German government, with Soviet approval, had set up a barbed-wire fence partitioning East Berlin and West Berlin to make it harder for East Germans to cross over to freedom. Soon the barbed wire was replaced by a massive wall that snaked nearly one hundred miles across the city, complete with machine-gun towers manned by guards with orders to kill anyone attempting to get over it. By the time Kennedy flew into Berlin on July 23, 1963, the Berlin Wall (or the "anti-fascist protective rampart," as it was officially known in East Germany) had become a symbol not only of the division of Germany, but a metaphor for the wider division of the free and communist worlds.

Two million people—two-thirds of West Berlin's population—cheered as Jack climbed to a platform outside the city hall on June 26. He delivered a stirring speech that he partly improvised on the spot:

LEFT In the shadow of the wall: Kennedy makes his famous "Ich bin ein Berliner" speech, June 26, 1963.

Two thousand years ago the proudest boast was civis Romanus sum *[I am a citizen of Rome]. Today, in the world of freedom, the proudest boast is* Ich bin ein Berliner *[I am a citizen of Berlin].*

There are many people in the world who really don't understand, or say they don't, what is the great issue between the free world and the communist world. Let them come to Berlin. There are some who say that communism is the wave of the future. Let them come to Berlin. And there are some who say in Europe and elsewhere we can work with the communists. Let them come to Berlin. And there are even a few who say that it is true that communism is an evil system, but it permits us to make economic progress. Lass' sie nach Berlin kommen. *Let them come to Berlin!*

The cheers were deafening. Aboard Air Force One en route to their next stop in Ireland, Jack told Ted Sorensen "We'll never have another day like this one."

Jack's triumph in Berlin was soon followed by a personal tragedy. At first, despite his philandering and the demands of his job, he and Jackie had tried to keep up something like a normal married life. But as the pressures of being the leader of the free world mounted, they spent less and less time together. When Jackie became pregnant in early 1963, the prospect of another child seemed to draw them closer together.

Jackie went into labor on August 7 in Massachusetts. Patrick Bouvier Kennedy was born almost six weeks prematurely and suffering from what's now known as Respiratory Distress Syndrome—he couldn't breathe on his own. Rushed to Boston's Children Hospital, he died two days later.

Jack and Jackie grieved deeply—and separately. It was two days before Jack could bring himself to even see Jackie. Not long afterward, she flew to Europe to recover in the company of her sister.

On September 24, the Senate ratified the Nuclear Test-Ban Treaty between the United States, Britain, and the Soviet Union by a margin of 80 to 19. The treaty was far from comprehensive: It didn't limit underground testing and it didn't prevent several other nations from developing nuclear weapons in the years ahead. But in Jack's words, the treaty was "a shaft of light" that pierced the gloom of the Cold War. He'd lost a son, but he'd indeed made the world a little safer for all other children.

A PLACE CALLED VIETNAM

Kennedy had plenty of domestic concerns on his mind as summer 1963 turned to fall. His civil rights initiative was flailing, and his proposal for a tax cut got the cold shoulder from Congress. The economy was in pretty good shape, but the stock market had fallen and unemployment had risen. Conservative businesspeople were upset by what they felt was the administration's inept response to an increase in steel prices in 1962. On top of all this, Kennedy had to start thinking about his reelection campaign in 1964. But there was another preoccupation, a situation on the other side of the world.

South Vietnam had replaced Laos as the Cold War's Southeast Asian "flash point." After France gave up its colonies in the region in the 1950s, Vietnam was partitioned into two states—communist

North Vietnam, led by Ho Chi Minh, and a pro–United States South Vietnam. Under an international

agreement, elections were supposed to be held to reunite the country and determine its form of gov-

ernment. These elections never took place. Around 1960, communist guerillas—the Vietcong—began

to operate in South Vietnam, with support and reinforcements from North Vietnam. In response, the

United States upped its commitment to protecting South Vietnam, sending weapons, military advisers,

aircraft, and other aid to the regime in Saigon.

Kennedy was somewhat wary of the increasing commitment of U.S. troops and resources in

Vietnam. Charles de Gaulle had warned him in 1961 that the conflict would prove to be a "quagmire."

Kennedy himself (a very moderate drinker) compared the ever-growing U.S. presence in Vietnam to

taking a drink: You take one, and then you have to take another to maintain the effect, and so on . . .

Nevertheless, Kennedy still adhered to the concept of the "domino effect" articulated by his

predecessor Dwight Eisenhower: If South Vietnam fell under communist control, neighboring nations

ABOVE The president signs the Nuclear Test-Ban Treaty in the White House's Treaty Room, October 7, 1963.

might topple, too, like a row of dominos. In August 1963, he told the ambassador to South Vietnam—
his former gubernatorial rival Henry Cabot Lodge—that "Anything that helps [the anticommunist
effort] we are in favor of, and anything that hinders it, we are opposed to."

The regime in Saigon that the United States was supporting was deeply unpopular with most
South Vietnamese. The president, Ngo Ding Diem, was spectacularly corrupt and brutal. He parceled
out the top government posts to his family, and the Diems—Catholics—antagonized the country's Buddhist majority. Several Buddhist monks publicly burned themselves to death in protest. Diem's sister-
in-law, Madame Nhu, referred to these as "happy barbecues."

ABOVE A map of South Vietnam dominates the background of a March 1961 press conference.

Kennedy was concerned about the global perception that the United States was supporting a repressive government just because it happened to be anticommunist. There seemed to be a solution to the problem of Diem. The administration learned that some of Diem's generals were planning a coup to overthrow him. The United States sent word that they wouldn't stand in the way of the coup. The coup went ahead on November 1. Despite assurances from the plotters that Diem and his family wouldn't be harmed, he and his brother-in-law were shot. Kennedy wept at the news.

Vietnam would become the scene of a long, costly war that deeply divided American society. One of history's great questions is whether Kennedy would have escalated the war or drawn down the U.S. commitment. His death in November of 1963 prevented us from knowing, though evidence exists that he planned at least a small-scale reduction of U.S. forces in the country in late 1963.

A DAY IN DALLAS

Three weeks after the anti-Diem coup, Kennedy embarked on a tour of Texas in the hopes of smoothing over infighting in the state's Democratic Party in preparation for the upcoming presidential campaign.

Dallas was on the itinerary. The city wasn't Kennedy country. It was home to some fire-breathing right-wingers who viewed the president as some kind of "commie." In October, Adlai Stevenson was actually spat on and physically attacked by an angry crowd when he made an appearance in the city.

Despite fears for his safety, Kennedy, Johnson, and their wives flew into Dallas's Love Field on Friday, November 22. Together with Texas Governor John Connally and his wife Nellie, Jack and Jackie clambered into the presidential limousine, a heavily modified Lincoln convertible. The Lincoln could be fitted with a bubble top, but Jack decided against using it (despite Jackie's wishes) and ordered the limo's bulletproof side windows rolled down. The limo joined twenty-four other cars in a motorcade destined for the city's Trade Mart, where Kennedy was scheduled to give a lunchtime speech.

Any fears seemed unfounded as the motorcade turned into Dealey Plaza around 12:30 p.m. The route was lined with thousands of cheering Texans. "You can't say that Dallas isn't friendly to you today," Nellie Connally said with a smile.

However, on the sixth floor of the Texas Schoolbook Depository, twenty-four-year-old Lee Harvey Oswald leaned out a window and aimed an old Italian bolt-action rifle he'd bought through the mail for $12.78.

Oswald was the very definition of a troubled loner. Raised by a single mother who moved frequently, he'd been diagnosed as showing "schizoid" tendencies at age fourteen. After he dropped out of high school, Oswald—by then a self-proclaimed Marxist—served in the Marines before renouncing his U.S. citizenship and defecting to the Soviet Union. He worked as a machinist in a factory in Minsk for a couple of years and married a Russian woman, but when the novelty of being an American in Russia wore off, he managed to get repatriated to America.

Oswald aimed the gun at Kennedy and pulled the trigger. His first shot probably went wild. He fired a second time, hitting Jack in the chest and throat—wounds he might have survived. The bullet

exited the president and wounded Governor Connally. The third bullet—maybe a ricochet—took off the back of Jack's head.

Sirens blaring, the motorcade tore off to Parkland Memorial Hospital. Doctors tried to resuscitate the president, but the head wound was too massive. He was declared dead at 1:00 p.m. News of Kennedy's death went out thirty minutes later. On factory floors, in offices, in classrooms, and on military bases around the world, Americans went into a collective state of shock and grief.

Air Force One flew back to Washington with Kennedy's body aboard. Lyndon Johnson took the Oath of Office as the thirty-sixth president aboard the plane, with a tearful Jackie, her dress splattered with her husband's blood, standing beside him.

After the shooting, Oswald left the Depository and retrieved his other gun, a pistol, from his boarding-house room. Confronted on the street by Dallas policeman J. D. Tippit, Oswald shot and killed Tippit and fled into a movie theater, where he was arrested.

On the following Saturday, Kennedy's casket lay in repose in the East Room of the White House before it was moved to the capitol to lie in state. Meanwhile, a handcuffed Oswald was led through the basement of the Dallas police headquarters for transfer to the county jail. Millions watched on live TV as Jack Ruby, a strip-club owner and petty criminal who nevertheless liked to pal around with cops, pulled out a .38 revolver and killed Oswald.

ABOVE Perhaps the last photograph of Kennedy alive, taken moments before Lee Harvey Oswald's shots rang out. RIGHT Cecil Stoughton, official White House photographer during the Kennedy years, was in Dallas and present to take this unforgettable of photograph of Lyndon Johnson being sworn in as president aboard Air Force One as Jackie looked on.

Kennedy's funeral took place that Monday. After a requiem mass at St. Matthew's Cathedral in Washington, D.C., the casket was carried down the steps and loaded on a horse-drawn caisson, followed by a riderless horse—the military symbol for a fallen commander.

A veiled Jackie leaned down and whispered in John's ear: "You can salute your daddy now, and say goodbye to him." John manfully raised his hand to his brow—burning an indelible image into America's memory.

The funeral procession continued to Arlington National Cemetery, where John F. Kennedy was laid to rest in a grave topped by an eternally burning flame.

ABOVE Jackie, John Jr., and Caroline, followed by Bobby, walk past the guard of honor at Jack's funeral. RIGHT The funeral procession crosses Memorial Bridge on its somber journey to Arlington National Cemetery.

the LEGACY

6.

IN THE WAKE OF Kennedy's assassination, the country was seized first by grief and then by incredulity. How could a "lone nut" like Oswald have managed to murder the president of the United States? In the aftermath of November 22, 1963, and to this day, millions of people became convinced that what happened on that terrible day in Dallas had to be the result of a conspiracy.

Only a week after Kennedy's death, Lyndon Johnson formed the President's Commission on the Death of President Kennedy, popularly known as the Warren Commission after its chairman, Chief Justice Earl Warren. Its report, issued eighteen months later, concluded that Oswald had acted alone. Many viewed the report as a rush to judgment intended to mislead and mollify the American people. In fact, *Rush to Judgment* became the title of a book by Mark Lane, one of the earliest assassination conspiracy theorists. Conspiracy theories have multiplied ever since.

Some believe it may have been the Mafia, who resented the loss of their lucrative gambling and prostitution operations in Cuba after Castro took over, and who resented Kennedy's failure to overthrow Castro. Or maybe the mob sought to send a very extreme message to Bobby Kennedy to back off

LEFT With the newly lit eternal flame flickering, Jackie kneels in prayer at Jack's grave. ABOVE Jack's body lies at the White House.

in his investigations of the labor unions they controlled. Others say it could have been a hit ordered by mob boss Sam Giancana seeking revenge for Jack's relationship with his mistress, Judith Campbell.

Other theories involve foreign governments. Cuba could have been seeking revenge for the Bay of Pigs and the Kennedy administration's attempts to assassinate Castro. A variation of this theory has the Cubans contracting the job to the Mafia. The Soviet government could have had the president killed in an effort to destabilize the U.S. government. Or elements of the South Vietnamese leadership could have been trying to get revenge for the coup that killed the Diem brothers.

Conspirators have also fingered Lyndon Johnson as the culprit, citing a desperate motive to move up to the top slot by any means necessary. Some say it could have been a cabal of the CIA, top U.S. military leaders, and defense-industry executives who feared that Kennedy would pull U.S. forces out of Vietnam or seek peace with the communist world, thereby undermining their influence on the government and cutting corporate profits. This idea was first put forward by New Orleans District Attorney Jim Garrison in 1966, and it became the basis of director Oliver Stone's 1991 movie *JFK*.

If there *wasn't* a conspiracy, theorists have countered their critics, then why did Oswald proclaim, "I'm just a patsy" after his arrest? What about Oswald's alleged association with various right- and left-wing groups? And wasn't it plausible that Jack Ruby, who may also have had ties to the Mafia, had been deliberately tasked with silencing Oswald?

People have also identified conflicting information between what really happened in Dealey Plaza and the "official version" of events: It seems impossible for Oswald to have gotten off his shots at that distance and within that timeframe. It would have taken a "magic bullet" to hit both Connally and Kennedy. Recordings at the scene recorded shots coming from other directions. A second gunman had been spotted on a "grassy knoll" in Dealey Plaza.

While theories abound, the consensus among reputable historians today is that Oswald did indeed act alone, even if the conclusions of the Warren Commission and subsequent official investigations were flawed. But in the absence of new evidence or new forensic technologies to apply against the existing evidence, speculation about the assassination will likely go on forever.

HONORED IN DEATH

America paid greater tribute to President Kennedy than to any other fallen chief executive, except perhaps Lincoln and Washington. All over the country, streets, avenues, roads, bridges, schools, and government buildings were named or renamed after John F. Kennedy. Idlewild International Airport in New York City became John F. Kennedy International Airport. Kennedy's profile went on the half-dollar coin in 1964. In 1967, the Navy's newest aircraft carrier, the USS *John F. Kennedy*, began the first of forty years of service. Jackie and Caroline christened the ship.

RIGHT Caroline swings a bottle of bubbly to christen the aircraft carrier *John F. Kennedy* at Newport News, Virginia, on May 27, 1967. It was a rare official appearance for Jackie.

Two such tributes were especially fitting. NASA's launch facility in Florida, Cape Canaveral, became the John F. Kennedy Space Center (now known as the Kennedy Space Center at Cape Canaveral). Kennedy's belief that the arts should be a major part of American life became physically embodied in 1971 when the John F. Kennedy Center for the Performing Arts, designed by architect Edward Durrell Stone, opened on the banks of the Potomac River in Washington.

The honors have not been limited to America. Belgium, Britain, Canada, Ireland, Israel, and many other countries also memorialized Jack in various ways. And in Berlin—which finally became the capital of a united, democratic Germany in 1990—the spot where Jack delivered his famous "Ich bin ein Berliner" speech—is now John F. Kennedy Platz.

A PLACE IN HISTORY

American historians are constantly asked to rate the country's presidents. In most such polls,

John F. Kennedy is deemed a "near-great" president. Historians cite his recklessness at the Bay of Pigs,

his hesitancy over civil rights, and his seeming inability to get major legislation passed by Congress

as reasons for not elevating him to "great" status. When members of the American public are polled,

however, they consistently put Kennedy into the "great" category.

Jack's popularity among the public certainly has something to do with the timeframe of his presi-

dency. His thousand-day administration was a period when many Americans couldn't locate Vietnam

on a map and when the social dislocations of the sixties were still to be confronted. In retrospect, the

Kennedy years became, in the words of Lerner and Loewe's Camelot song, "one brief shining moment"

before the nation entered one of its most turbulent and divisive eras. Jack's youth, his wit, and his opti-

mism all fit the temper of the times.

ABOVE The Capitol is illuminated as thousands line up to view the body of the assassinated president lying
in state. RIGHT This photo captures an image of the handsome thirty-fifth president with his striking wife in
their radiant youthful days, circa 1953.

It didn't take long before the cracks in Camelot's walls became evident. Starting in the late 1960s and continuing to this day, biographies, memoirs, investigative journalism, and official investigations revealed what went on behind the castle walls. Revelations of Jack's womanizing, his illnesses and drug use, the administration's collusion in unsavory activities like Operation Mongoose and the coup against Diem have come to light. Some historians have suggested that if Jack had lived and been reelected, he wouldn't have survived another term: His illnesses might have killed him, or disclosures about his infidelities might have led to his impeachment.

And yet while these revelations tarnished Jack's posthumous reputation, they didn't fully diminish the luster of his time in office.

THE SUCCESSORS

In the White House at last, Lyndon Johnson lost no time in making his mark. In November 1964, he won the presidency in his own right, crushing the arch-conservative Republican nominee Barry Goldwater in a historic landslide. In 1964 and 1965, he signed two historic pieces of civil rights legislation into law, the Voting Rights Act and the Civil Rights Act, respectively. In signing these acts, Johnson achieving what his predecessor had worked so hard to accomplish during the last year of his presidency. He launched a "war on poverty" and announced his intention to build a Great Society in America, fueled by massive infusions of federal money into education, health care, and community development.

The United States was still in the midst of the Cold War, and the front line was now Vietnam. After a mysterious episode in which North Vietnamese patrol boats attacked a couple of U.S. Navy destroyers, Congress passed the Gulf of Tonkin Resolution, essentially giving the president a blank check to wage war. Johnson responded with a bombing campaign against North Vietnam in late 1964 and the dispatch of the first regular combat troops to South Vietnam in the spring of 1965. By 1967, more than a half-million Americans were fighting in Vietnam.

As the war dragged on and casualties mounted, Vietnam became an increasingly divisive issue at home, and Johnson's popularity began to wane. Still, most observers expected him to run for another term. (Having succeeded to the presidency upon his predecessor's death, Johnson was exempt from the Twenty-Second Amendment's two-term limit.) Instead, he stunned the nation with a twofold announcement: The United States would halt their bombing of North Vietnam, and he would not be a presidential candidate in 1968. Johnson died of a heart attack at his Texas ranch only five years later, in 1973.

The 1968 Democratic National Convention was tumultuous, with antiwar protestors clashing with police on the streets of Chicago. The Democratic nomination eventually went to Johnson's

LEFT President at last, Lyndon Johnson signs the Civil Rights Act of 1964 into law on July 2. "Well, we [the Democrats] have lost the South for a generation," he reportedly said as he signed the bill.

vice president, Hubert Humphrey. Humphrey was up against none other than Kennedy's quasi-friend turned rival, Richard Nixon.

Just a few years earlier, a Nixon candidacy had seemed unthinkable. After his defeat in 1960, he'd been written off as a political factor following a failed bid for California's governorship in 1962. But the nation had changed a lot since then. The forces that had begun stirring during Kennedy's administration erupted into a national convulsion during the Johnson years. Vietnam turned many of the idealistic baby boomers who revered Kennedy into cynics. Young men burned their draft cards or fled abroad to avoid military service. Protests against the war proliferated. A new sixties counterculture promoted drug use, defiance of traditional sexual morality, and a general spirit of questioning authority. Despite the gains of the civil rights movement, many African Americans still found themselves at the bottom of the heap when it came to jobs, education, and housing. Riots swept many of the nation's cities, especially in the wake of Martin Luther King Jr.'s assassination in April 1968.

All this frightened many Americans, and Nixon shrewdly played to this fear. In his nomination acceptance speech, he appealed to the "Great Silent Majority" of Americans for support. He also promised "peace with honor" in Vietnam. These promises won him the White House in 1968, and he went on to reelection in 1972. It wasn't until 1973 that the last U.S. troops left Vietnam. Two years later, North Vietnamese forces swept southward and reunited the country under communist rule. By that time, Nixon had resigned office in disgrace after the Watergate scandal.

THE PARENTS

Just thirteen months after seeing Jack sworn in, Joe Sr. suffered a massive stroke that left him paralyzed on his right side and, at first, unable to speak. His mind was still keen, though, and on November 22, 1963, he must have recognized that something was deeply wrong from the commotion around the Hyannis Port compound. The next day Eunice and Teddy broke the news to him. Joe Sr. lived on until November 18, 1969, by which time he'd mourned the loss of a third son.

Jack's death triggered a rare crisis of faith in Rose. She later wrote of how she'd paced up and down the beach at Hyannis Port after hearing the news: "Everything was lost, and I wondered why." She would live until January 18, 1995, when pneumonia claimed her at the astonishing age of 104.

THE BROTHERS

Bobby was shattered by his brother's death. Despite his own accomplishments, he'd always put his brother's career first, and with Jack gone, in Lem Billings's words, "He didn't know where he was. . . . Everything was just pulled out from under him."

RIGHT Ted Kennedy (left), senator from Massachusetts, with his older brother Bobby, senator from New York, during budget hearings in 1967.

He initially stayed on as attorney general under Johnson, but the contentious relationship between the two ensured that was only a temporary arrangement. Finding solace in ancient and modern philosophy texts and mountain climbing, Bobby made the decision to continue Jack's legacy by entering elective politics. After establishing residency in New York, he won a Senate seat in 1964. By some accounts, he was considering a bid for the 1968 Democratic presidential nomination as early as 1965.

By now Bobby was a changed man. His old intensity remained, but much of his abrasiveness vanished, and he developed a deep empathy for the poor and marginalized in American society. He'd seen firsthand the effects of poverty and lack of opportunity in places ranging from the urban slums of New York City to the hills and hollows of Appalachia. He wanted to do something about it. He was also growing increasingly opposed to Johnson's vast expansion of the war in Vietnam.

Even though he wasn't officially a candidate, Bobby won—albeit narrowly—the New Hampshire primary in March 1968. A couple of days later, he formally announced his candidacy: "I do not run for the Presidency merely to oppose any man, but to propose new policies. I run because I am convinced that this country is on a perilous course and because I have such strong feelings about what must be done, and I feel that I'm obliged to do all I can."

On June 4, 1968, Bobby won the California primary, putting him in a good position against his rivals, Vice President Hubert Humphrey and Wisconsin Senator Eugene McCarthy. After celebrating the victory at the Ambassador Hotel in Los Angeles, Bobby exited through the kitchen so he could shake hands with the workers. One of them, a Jordanian immigrant named Sirhan B. Sirhan, pulled out a revolver and fired three shots into Bobby at close range. Bobby died the following morning. As with his older brother's assassination, conspiracy theories have abounded about Sirhan's motivation, but the likeliest of explanations is Bobby's support for Israel. After a funeral at New York's St. Patrick's Cathedral, Bobby joined Jack beneath the eternal flame at Arlington.

With Joe Jr., Jack, and Bobby now gone, Teddy was next in the line of succession of the closest thing to an American royal family. But Ted had some problems hitting the high marks set by his older brothers except in football. He threw the only touchdown pass for Harvard in the 1955 Harvard–Yale game, and he was scouted professionally. Ted had been suspended from Harvard in 1951 for cheating on an exam, but after serving in the Army, he was readmitted and graduated in 1956. In 1960, Ted was elected to the U.S. Senate, but because he hadn't reached the constitutionally required age of thirty, he didn't take his seat until 1962. Massachusetts voters have returned him to the Senate ever since, and at the publication of this book, he is the nation's second-longest-serving senator.

Ted's chances of reaching the White House may have been doomed on the night of July 18, 1969. Driving home from a party with Mary Jo Kopechne, a young woman who'd worked on Bobby's presidential campaign, Ted's car went off a bridge on Chappaquiddick Island, Massachusetts, and into the water. Kennedy managed to get out of the car. Kopechne did not, and it wasn't until the next day that Ted informed the police. He was charged with leaving the scene of an accident and given a two-month suspended sentence. Many Americans felt the absurdly lenient sentence was due only to the power of Kennedy's name.

Ted did not actively pursue the Democratic presidential nomination until 1980, and he eventually withdrew his candidacy in support of the incumbent president, Jimmy Carter. In the Senate, Ted continued as a bastion of his party's liberal wing, even as the country moved farther to the right after Ronald Reagan's election in 1980.

In May 2008, Ted was diagnosed with brain cancer, for which he underwent surgery the following month. Despite his illness, Ted flew to the Democratic National Convention in Denver that August, where Barack Obama—born in the first year of Jack's presidency—secured the party's nomination. In his speech to the convention, Ted invoked his brother's inaugural address: "This November, the torch will be passed again to a new generation of Americans. So, with Barack Obama and for you and for me, our country will be committed to his cause. The work begins anew. The hope rises again. And the dream lives on." The torch was passed with Obama's victory in November 2008.

JACKIE KENNEDY ONASSIS

Jackie's courage and composure during the assassination and its aftermath captured the hearts of America and the world. Beneath the façade, though, she was, in Theodore White's words, "without tears, drained, white of face." In the space of a decade, she'd gone from being a carefree photojournalist to the wife of a senator to the widow of a murdered president. She was only thirty-four years old.

For a year after Jack's death, she lived in virtual seclusion in Virginia, in a house she and Jack had picked out to serve as their postpresidential home, before moving to a Fifth Avenue apartment in New York City. She continued to keep a low profile, appearing occasionally at official ceremonies connected with her late husband. She began a successful career as a book editor, first at the Viking Press and then at Doubleday. In her spare time, she supported historic preservation efforts: she's credited with helping save New York's Grand Central Station from the wrecking ball. As she had done in the White House, she zealously guarded Caroline and John Jr.'s privacy.

ABOVE Jackie at the office during her first day on the job as an editor at the Viking Press, September 22, 1975.

Jackie remained close to Bobby, and his death in June 1968 devastated her anew and left her bitter and fearful. "I despise America," she told Pierre Salinger, who'd been Jack's press secretary. "If they're killing Kennedys in this country, my kids are number one targets. I want to get my children out of this country."

Three months later, she remarried, to Aristotle Onassis, a Greek shipping tycoon. The marriage shocked and dismayed many Americans: How could the queen of Camelot consent to become the consort of a foreigner more than twenty years her senior?

Jackie had inherited her mother's insecurity about money. After her wedding to Jack, for example, she sold many of their wedding presents—something which angered Jack. Onassis was one of the world's richest people. Their prenuptial agreement guaranteed Jackie that she would never have to worry about money again. In any event, the couple didn't spend much time together. He died in 1975. She never married again, although businessman Maurice Tempelsman became her constant companion in later years.

In early 1994, Jackie was diagnosed with non-Hodgkin's lymphoma, succumbing to the disease on May 19 at the age of sixty-four.

ABOVE With Bobby and Ted in support, Jackie prepares to make her first public statement on January 14, 1964, almost fourteen months after Jack's assassination. RIGHT Ted, Caroline, John Jr., and Jackie at a press conference at the John F. Kennedy Library and Museum in Boston, Massachusetts, May 1989.

THE CHILDREN

After graduating from Harvard and earning a law degree from Columbia, Caroline pursued a career as an attorney. She married Edward Schlossberg in 1986 and at the publication of this book, the couple has three children. Caroline works with various organizations connected with her father's legacy, including the Profiles in Courage Award, given annually to elected officials demonstrating independence and conviction despite public opinion and political expediency. Her strong interest in civil liberties led her to cowrite two books, *In Our Defense: The Bill of Rights in Action* (1990) and *The Right to Privacy* (1995), and to edit popular works like the anthology *A Patriot's Handbook: Poems, Stories, and Speeches Celebrating the Land We Love* (2003). In 2008, she served on Barack Obama's vice-presidential selection committee, and she introduced her Uncle Teddy at the party's national convention. When Hilary Clinton accepted the post of Secretary of State in President Barack Obama's cabinet, many thought Caroline to be the leading candidate for appointment as New York senator, but she withdrew her name from contention.

As the prince of Camelot, John F. Kennedy Jr. grew to manhood with many expecting him to continue his father's legacy. Like his father, however, John Jr. seemed hesitant about a career in elective politics. Breaking with family tradition, he graduated from Brown University, instead of Harvard, with an English degree, and he went on to earn his law degree from New York University. He won admittance to the New York Bar after three tries.

He served as an assistant district attorney in Manhattan from 1989 to 1993 before leaving law to found *George*, a glossy political magazine with the slogan "Not Just Politics as Usual." In 1996, he married Carolyn Bessette, a model and publicist. Despite their efforts to stay out of the limelight, the handsome couple became a gossip column staple.

Aviation had fascinated Jack. John Jr. took it a step further by becoming a private pilot. On July 16, 1999, John took off from Essex County Airport in New Jersey with Carolyn and her sister

aboard his Piper Saratoga, bound for a wedding in Hyannis Port. They never arrived. After four days of recovery efforts, search crews found the plane's wreckage and all three bodies in the waters of Martha's Vineyard. The cause of the crash has never been conclusively determined. John was thirty-eight.

To many Americans, John Jr.'s death marked the moment when the light that illuminated the "brief shining moment . . . that was Camelot" finally went dark.

Flawed as he was as a person and as a president, John F. Kennedy still touched a chord in the American people that still resonates in a new century. He inspired Americans to strive for excellence as individuals, and he urged the nation as a whole to live up to its ideals and serve as an example for the world. The themes that marked his presidency will remain his enduring legacy for as long as Americans respond to his call, "Ask not what your country can do for you—ask what you can do for your country."

ABOVE The first family at the White House, with Caroline's arm around her father's shoulder. This photo was taken in November 1963, just before Jack's death shattered the family forever. RIGHT At the 1964 Democratic National Convention in Atlantic City, Jack was given tribute by his brother Bobby: "When there were periods of crisis, you stood beside him. When there were periods of happiness, you laughed with him. And when there were periods of sorrow, you comforted him."

CREDITS

Every effort has been made to trace copyright holders. If any unintended omissions have been made, becker&mayer! would be pleased to add appropriate acknowledgment in future editions.

All images, documents, and audio tracks are courtesy of the John F. Kennedy Presidential Library & Museum, with the exception of the following:

Page 2: © Bettmann/Corbis

Page 6: AP Images

Page 10 (left): © John F. Kennedy
     Library Foundation

Page 23: © John F. Kennedy Library Foundation

Page 25: © John F. Kennedy Library Foundation

Page 30: © William Hustler and Georgina Hustler

Page 33: © John F. Kennedy Library Foundation

Page 43: © Bettmann/Corbis

Page 45 (photo): © John F. Kennedy
     Library Foundation

Page 46: © John F. Kennedy Library Foundation

Page 76: Morgan Collection/Getty Images

Page 78: © Bettmann/Corbis

Page 84: Arnold Newman/Getty Images

Page 86: Hank Walker/Time Life Pictures/
     Getty Images

Page 91: © Eddie Germano

Page 92: © Bettmann/Corbis

Page 93: © Bettmann/Corbis

Page 101: © Bettmann/Corbis

Page 103 (right top and bottom): Joel Benjamin
     and JFK Library Foundation

Page 106: © Bettmann/Corbis

Page 107 (photo): © Bettmann/Corbis

Page 107 (ticket and brochure): Joel Benjamin
     and JFK Library Foundation

Page 108: © Bettmann/Corbis

Page 109: © Bettmann/Corbis

Page 112: Paul Schutzer/Time Life Pictures/
     Getty Images

Page 116: © Bettmann/Corbis

Page 137: © Bettmann/Corbis

Page 143: Stan Wayman/Time Life Pictures/
     Getty Images

Page 152: © Bettmann/Corbis

Page 154: Central Press/Getty Images

Page 155: © Bettmann/Corbis

Page 156: © Bettmann/Corbis

Page 157: AP Images

Page 159: © Bettmann/Corbis

Page 160: © Bettmann/Corbis

Page 162: © Bettmann/Corbis

Page 165: © Bettmann/Corbis

Page 167: © Bettmann/Corbis

Page 168: © Bettmann/Corbis

Page 169: © Bettmann/Corbis

LEFT Jack was never happier than when he was on the water. Here, he and Jackie watch the 1962 America's Cup yacht race. PAGE 175 Jack and Caroline, August 1963.

BIBLIOGRAPHY

BOOKS

Avedon, Richard, and Shannon Thomas Perich. *The Kennedys: Portrait of a Family.* New York: Collins
   Design, 2007.

Dallek, Robert. *John F. Kennedy: An Unfinished Life, 1917–1963.* New York: Little, Brown & Co., 2003.

Goodwin, Doris Kearns. *The Fitzgeralds and the Kennedys: An American Saga.* New York: Simon &
   Schuster, 2001.

Hamilton, Nigel. *JFK: Reckless Youth.* New York: Random House, 1992.

Horowitz, David, and Peter Collier. *The Kennedys: An American Drama.* New York: Simon &
   Schuster, 1985.

Maier, Thomas. *The Kennedys: America's Emerald Kings.* New York: Basic Books, 2004.

O'Brien, Michael. *John F. Kennedy: A Biography.* New York: Thomas Dunne, 2005.

Perret, Geoffrey. *Jack: A Life Like No Other.* New York: Random House, 2002.

Reeves, Richard. *President Kennedy: Profile of Power.* New York: Simon & Schuster, 1994.

Schlesinger, Arthur M., Jr. *A Thousand Days: John F. Kennedy in the White House.* Boston: Mariner
   Books, 2002.

Sorensen, Ted (compiler). *Let the Word Go Forth: The Speeches, Statements, and Writings of John F.
   Kennedy 1947 to 1963.* New York: Delacourt, 1988.

Talbot, David. *Brothers: The Hidden History of the Kennedy Years.* Boston: Free Press, 2008.

INTERNET

John F. Kennedy Presidential Library and Museum: www.jfklibrary.org

AUDIO

Dallek, Robert and Terry Golway. *Let Every Nation Know* (book with audio CD). Sourcebooks
   MediaFusion, 2007.

Live Recordings. *John F. Kennedy: The Kennedy Wit* (audio CD). Speechworks, 1999.

DVD

Biography: *JFK: A Personal Story.* A&E DVD Archives, 1997.

History Channel: *JFK: A Presidency Revealed.* A&E Home Video, 2003.

ABOUT THE AUTHOR

A former publishing executive, Chuck Wills is now a writer, editor, and consultant specializing in American history. His recent books include *Destination America*, a history of immigration to the United States (a companion volume to the PBS series of the same name); *America's Presidents*; *Lincoln: The Presidential Archives*; *The Thomas Jefferson Portfolio*; and a children's biography of Annie Oakley. Wills lives in New York City.

ACKNOWLEDGMENTS

The author wishes to thank all the great people at becker&mayer!, especially his superbly skilled, patient, and good-humored editor, Meghan Cleary. Many thanks also to photo researcher Shayna Ian for a thorough and thoughtful job, designer Paul Barrett for the elegant layout, and production coordinator Shirley Woo. In addition, the author would like to thank his friends and family for all their support, in so many ways, during the writing of this book.